HEALING YOUR
TRAUMATIZED HEART

D0395696

Companion Press is dedicated to the education and support of both the bereaved and bereavement caregivers.

We believe that those who companion the bereaved by walking with them as they journey in grief have a wondrous opportunity: to help others embrace and grow through grief and to lead fuller, more deeply-lived lives themselves because of this important work.

HEALING YOUR TRAUMATIZED HEART:

•

100 PRACTICAL IDEAS
AFTER SOMEONE YOU LOVE DIES
A SUDDEN, VIOLENT DEATH

•

ALAN D. WOLFELT, PH.D.

Companion
PRESS

Fort Collins, Colorado

An imprint of the Center for Loss and Life Transition

Companion Press is an imprint of the
Center for Loss and Life Transition,
3735 Broken Bow Road, Fort Collins, Colorado 80526

Companion Press books may be purchased in bulk for sales promotions, premiums or fundraisers. Please contact the publisher at the above address for more information.

Printed in the United States of America

11 10 09 08 07 06 05 04 03 02   5 4 3 2 1

ISBN: 1-879651-32-7

In memory of the 3,056 victims of the World Trade Center, Pentagon and United Flight 93 attacks and in support of those who love and miss them.

INTRODUCTION

One year ago, on one tragic day, 3,056 people died suddenly and violently in the attacks on the World Trade Center, the Pentagon and United Flight 93 in Pennsylvania. In the years before the September 11th attacks, hundreds of others were killed by the bombing of the Alfred P. Murrah Federal Building in Oklahoma City and the 1999 shootings at Columbine High School in Littleton, Colorado.

This book is for the families and friends devastated by events such as these. But it is also for those affected by more commonplace, less publicized—but equally traumatic—types of sudden, violent death—accidental death, homicide, suicide and deaths due to military action and natural disaster.

Did you know that more than 43,000 Americans die in motor vehicle crashes each year? That more than 29,000 complete suicide? In Canada, the suicide rate per 100,000 people is even higher, with more than 3,500 people completing suicide annually. Tragically, homicide accounts for the deaths of 17,000 Americans each year. More than 8,000 Canadians die every year as the result of an accident. And in the United States, more than 16,000 die each year from falls alone. Together, more than 160,000 Americans and Canadians die each year as a result of sudden, violent death. And because we know that most deaths intimately affect many people, this figure of 160,000 per year translates into millions of North Americans who've been traumatized by the sudden, violent death of someone close to them in the last decade. Multiplied worldwide, this number burgeons to hundreds of millions.

You are among them. You are a single human being who has been traumatized by the sudden, violent death of a family member, a friend, a coworker, a neighbor or someone else whose life touched yours. The event in which your loved one died may not have been epic in scale or considered media-worthy, but it was certainly traumatic nonetheless.

You are now struggling with both the traumatic nature of the death and your grief over the loss. For purposes of this book, trauma can be defined as an event of such intensity, brutality or magnitude of horror that it would overwhelm any human being's capacity to cope. You have been traumatized, which is essentially a normal response to an extreme event.

Naturally, traumatized mourners often find themselves replaying and reconsidering over and over the circumstances of the death. This is both normal and necessary. Such replay helps you begin to acknowledge the reality of the death and integrate it into your life. It is as if your mind needs to devote time and energy to comprehending the circumstances of the death before it can move on to confronting the fact that someone you love has died and will never be present to you again.

Post-traumatic stress disorder, or PTSD, is a term used to describe the psychological condition that survivors of sudden, violent death sometimes experience. People with PTSD often have nightmares or scary thoughts about the terrible experience they or their loved one went through. They try to stay away from anything that reminds them of the frightening experience. They often feel angry and are unable to care about or trust other people. They are often on the lookout for danger and get very upset when something happens without warning. Their anxiety level is continually high. The more you learn about trauma and PTSD, the more you will have some sense of control at a time when you naturally feel out of control. Knowledge is one of the best antidotes to anxiety, fear and depression.

If you think you may have PTSD, talk to your family doctor or a counselor. You may need therapy and/or medication for a time to help you feel safer and cope with your day-to-day life. You will need to get help for your PTSD before you can deal with grief and mourning.

It may be helpful for you to know that your response to trauma and the potential onset of PTSD symptoms has more to do with the intensity and duration of the stressful event in your life than with your personality. Don't think you are "weak" because this traumatic event and its repercussions have overwhelmed your coping resources. Don't feel ashamed if you need professional help.

But many of you are traumatized without having full-blown PTSD. You may have anxiety and anger. You may think about the circumstances of the death a lot. You may be in great pain. But if you are still able to function in your daily life and interact lovingly with others, you may not have the actual disorder called PTSD. Still, you are traumatized and in need of special care and consideration, both from yourself and from others.

The traumatic nature of the death and your thoughts and feelings about it will color every aspect of your grief. It is part of your grief. But it is not the totality of your grief. Other factors that contribute to your grief include the nature of the relationship you had with the person who died, your unique personality, your religious and cultural backgrounds, your gender, your age, your previous experiences with loss, as well as others. Your grief is a complicated blend of thoughts and emotions, most of which stem from your love for the person who died. Over time you will come to find that your grief is as much or more about the life than it is about the death.

Most books about trauma loss and PTSD are written for professional mental health caregivers, but this book is just for you!

It was written to help you embrace your grief in positive, proactive ways and to companion you on the journey to reconciliation. It contains 100 practical thoughts and ideas to help you understand your grief and, even more important, to express it. Grief expressed is called *mourning*, and mourning helps you heal. Grief repressed leads to chronic emotional, spiritual and physical problems.

I invite you to flip this book open to any page. Read through the Idea you encounter and determine if it speaks to your unique grief journey. If it doesn't, try another Idea. If it does, try the exercise described in the carpe diem (which means, as you know, seize the day). The carpe diem exercises are there to help you *do* something with your grief, right here and now, empowering you to be an active participant in your own healing.

And if you are able to muster the courage to actively mourn, you will heal. And you will grow. And you will love and live again. Remember, you are not alone. Millions of others have not only survived the traumatic death of a loved one, they've chosen to truly live. Find ways to reach out to these people. Find ways to share your experience. Find ways to make connections.

God bless you. I hope we meet one day.

Alan D. Wolfelt

1.

UNDERSTAND WHAT IT MEANS TO BE "TRAUMATIZED."

- You've been traumatized by a sudden and violent death. How is this different from your reaction to an anticipated or non-violent death? As you know, the death of someone loved always causes painful feelings. But in the case of sudden, violent death, your mind has an especially difficult time acknowledging and absorbing the circumstances of the death itself.

- In this sense, the word "trauma" refers to intense feelings of shock, fear, anxiety and helplessness surrounding the cause of death. Trauma is caused by events of such intensity or magnitude of horror that they would overwhelm any human being's capacity to cope.

- Certainly it can be said that death is always traumatic. Even the natural death of an aged parent can feel traumatic to her children. But sudden and violent deaths result in a kind of psychic injury and typically involve the creation of frightening and often intrusive thoughts about the distressful event that caused the death.

CARPE DIEM:
If you have grieved the death of someone loved before, consider how your feelings are different this time. How has the traumatic nature of the death shaped your grief?

2.

SEEK SAFETY AND COMFORT.

• After a traumatic experience, it's natural to feel vulnerable, unsafe and anxious. Your nervous system is telling your brain that the world isn't a safe place right now. Something violent has happened and, you naturally think, it could happen again.

• To overcome your trauma, you must locate yourself among people and in places that make you feel safe. If this means moving in with a friend or relative temporarily, that's OK. If this means avoiding certain places or people, that's OK, too.

• What calms and comforts you? Taking a walk? Cuddling with someone you love? Hugging your pet? Relaxing in the tub? Yoga or meditation or prayer? Identify activities that soothe you and turn to them when your anxiety is high.

• You will not be able to mourn if you feel unsafe or overly anxious. Seek safety and comfort first, then you can begin to slowly embrace your grief.

CARPE DIEM:
Let someone else take care of you today. It's normal and natural to need help with the activities of daily living in the early days and weeks after a traumatic death.

3.

UNDERSTAND THE DIFFERENCE BETWEEN GRIEF AND MOURNING.

- Grief is the constellation of internal thoughts and feelings we have when someone loved dies. Grief is the container for our experience of loss. This container is stored within us.

- Mourning is the outward expression of grief, including traumatic thoughts and feelings.

- Everyone grieves when someone loved dies, but if we are to heal, we must also mourn.

- Many of the ideas in this book are intended to help you mourn this death, to express your feelings of trauma and grief outside of yourself. Over time and with the support of others, to mourn is to heal.

- Mourn the death while remaining sensitive to your unique needs as a trauma survivor. You will need to be very self-compassionate and patient with yourself in the months and years to come. Give yourself the gift of time. While time alone doesn't heal wounds, healing does take time.

CARPE DIEM:
Ask yourself this: Have I been mourning this death or
have I restricted myself to grieving?

4.

UNDERSTAND THAT GRIEF FOLLOWING TRAUMA IS PARTICULARLY DIFFICULT.

- Not only has someone you care about died, but the death was sudden and violent. The traumatic aspects of the death will likely make your grief journey especially painful.

- As we've said, grief is the collection of thoughts and feelings you have on the inside after someone dies. This includes the thoughts and feelings you have about the death itself. Because the death was sudden and violent, this aspect of your grief may consume most of your energies, especially in the early weeks and months following the death.

- Even much later, after you've come to terms with the nature of the death, it will always be a significant part of your grief.

- Remember that just as your feelings of grief need to be expressed, so do your feelings of trauma. Your trauma is part of your grief and also needs to be mourned.

- Keep in mind that "healing" your trauma loss and "curing" your trauma loss are two different concepts. Healing is an active emotional and spiritual process in which you seek to be whole again. Curing is a medical term that implies that someone or something outside of you rids you of your grief. Your grief cannot be "cured;" it will always live inside you.

CARPE DIEM:
Find a trusted friend with whom to discuss the difference between "healing" and "curing."

5.

ALLOW FOR NUMBNESS.

- Feelings of shock, numbness and disbelief are nature's way of temporarily protecting us from the full reality of a sudden, violent death. They help us survive our early grief.

- We often think, "I will wake up and this will not have happened." Mourning can feel like being in a dream.

- Your emotions need time to catch up with what your mind has been told.

- Even after you have moved beyond these initial feelings, don't be surprised if they reemerge. Birthdays, holidays and anniversaries often trigger these normal and necessary feelings.

- Trauma loss often goes beyond what we consider "normal" shock. In fact, you may experience what is called "psychic numbing"—the deadening or shutting off of emotions. Your sense that "this isn't happening to me" may persist for months, sometimes even years. Don't set rigid expectations for yourself and your ability to function "normally" in the world around you.

- Think of shock and numbness as a bandage that your psyche has placed over your wound. The bandage protects the wound until it becomes less open and raw. Only after healing has begun and a scab forms is the bandage removed and the wound openly exposed to the world.

CARPE DIEM:
If you're feeling numb, cancel any commitments that require concentration and decision-making. Allow yourself time to regroup.

6.

STAY IN TOUCH WITH YOUR FEELINGS.

• You will probably feel many different feelings in the coming weeks and months. You may feel, among other things, numb, angry, guilty, afraid, confused and, of course, deeply sad. Sometimes these feelings follow each other within a short period of time or they may occur simultaneously.

• As strange as some of these emotions may seem to you, they are normal. Your feelings are what they are. They are not right or wrong, they simply are.

• Allow yourself to feel whatever it is you are feeling without judging yourself.

• Stay in touch with your feelings by leaning into them when you are ready. If you feel angry, for example, allow yourself to feel and think through this anger. Don't suppress it or distract yourself from it. Instead, acknowledge your feelings and give them voice. Tell a friend, "I feel so mad today because ..." or write in your journal, "I feel such regret that..."

• Learning to name your feelings will help you tame them. As Shakespeare's Macbeth reminded us, "Give sorrow words: the grief that does not speak whispers the o'er-fraught heart, and bids it break."

CARPE DIEM:
Using old magazines, clip images that capture the many feelings you've been having since the death. Make a "feelings collage" on poster board and display it somewhere you'll be able to reflect on it.

7.

CONSIDER YOURSELF IN "EMOTIONAL INTENSIVE CARE."

- Something catastrophic has happened in your life. Something assaulting to the very core of your being. Something excruciatingly painful.

- Your spirit has been deeply injured. Just as your body could not be expected to recover immediately from a brutal attack, neither can your psyche.

- Imagine that you've suffered a severe physical injury and are in your hospital's intensive care unit. Your friends and family surround you with their presence and love. The medical staff attends to you constantly. Your body rests and recovers.

- This is the kind of care you need and deserve right now. The blow you have suffered is no less devastating than this imagined physical injury. Allow others to take care of you. Ask for their help. Give yourself as much resting time as possible. Take time off work. Let household chores slide. In the early weeks and months after the death, don't expect—indeed, don't try—to carry on with your normal routine.

CARPE DIEM:

Close your eyes and imagine yourself in "emotional intensive care." Where are you? What kind of care are you receiving? From whom? Arrange a weekend or a week of the emotional and spiritual intensive care you most need.

8.

BE AWARE THAT YOUR GRIEF AFFECTS YOUR BODY, HEART, SOCIAL SELF AND SPIRIT.

• Grief is physically demanding. This is especially true with traumatic grief. Your body responds to the stress of the encounter and the immune system can weaken. You may be more susceptible to illness and physical discomforts. You may also feel lethargic, weak or highly fatigued. You may not be sleeping well and you may have no appetite. Your stomach may hurt. Your chest may ache.

• The emotional toll of grief is complex and painful. You may feel many different feelings, and those feelings can shift and blur over time.

• Bereavement naturally results in social discomfort. Friends and family may withdraw from you, leaving you isolated and unsupported.

• You may ask yourself, "Why go on living?" "Will my life have meaning now?" "Where is God in this?" Spiritual questions such as these are natural and necessary but also draining.

• Basically, your grief may affect every aspect of your life. Nothing may feel "normal" right now. If this is true for you, don't be alarmed. Just trust that in time, you will find peace and comfort again.

CARPE DIEM:
If you've felt physically affected by your grief, see a doctor this week. Sometimes it's comforting to receive a clean bill of health. Or, if you need some physical care, get it. Remember, your body is sometimes smarter than your head; it will let you know you have "special needs."

9.

ALLOW FOR FEELINGS OF UNFINISHED BUSINESS.

- Sudden death often brings about feelings of unfinished business. Things we never did, things we didn't get to say, things we wish we hadn't said.

- Allow yourself to think and feel through these "if onlys." You may never be able to fully resolve these issues, but if you permit yourself to mourn them, you will be become reconciled to them.

- Is there something you wanted to say to the person who died but never did? Write her a letter that openly expresses your thoughts and feelings.

CARPE DIEM:
Perhaps the person who died left some task incomplete.
Finish it on her behalf.

10.

BE COMPASSIONATE WITH YOURSELF.

- The journey through traumatic grief is a long and especially difficult one—maybe the most difficult life offers. It is also a journey for which there is no preparation.

- Be compassionate with yourself as you encounter traumatic thoughts and feelings. Do what you have to do to survive the coming weeks and months.

- Don't judge yourself or try to set a particular course for healing. You are NOT going crazy and there is no one right way to do this.

- When you were a child your parents probably told you that if you got lost, you should stay put. Don't go anywhere. Wait. Wait and call out for help. This is also good advice for grieving.

- Let your grief journey be what it is. And let yourself—your new, grieving self—be who you are.

CARPE DIEM:
Share some quiet time with someone wonderful in your life. Let that person know how important he is to you.

11.

TAKE GOOD CARE OF YOURSELF.

- Good self-care is nurturing and necessary for mourners, yet it's something many of us completely overlook.

- Try very hard to eat well and get adequate rest. Lay your body down 2-3 times a day for 20-30 minutes, even if you don't sleep. I know— you probably don't care very much about eating well right now, and you may be sleeping poorly. But taking care of yourself is truly one way to fuel healing and to begin to embrace life again.

- Listen to what your body tells you. "Get some rest," it says. "But I don't have time," you reply. "I have things to do." "OK, then, I'll get sick so you HAVE to rest," your body says. And it will get sick if that's what it takes to get its needs met!

- Drink at least 5-6 glasses of water each day. Dehydration can compound feelings of fatigue and disorientation.

- Exercise not only provides you with more energy, it can give you focused thinking time. Take a 20-minute walk every day. Or, if that seems too much, a five-minute walk. But don't over-exercise, because your body needs extra rest, as well.

- Now more than ever, you need to allow time for you.

CARPE DIEM:
Are you taking a multi-vitamin? If not, now is
probably a good time to start.

12.

DON'T TAKE ON ADDITIONAL STRESSES RIGHT NOW.

- Your plate is full right now—emotionally, spiritually, and physically. Now is not the time to take on additional stress in the form of increased work load, new commitments, elective life changes, etc.

- If you can (and I realize this isn't always possible), try to avoid making any major decisions for at least a year following the death. Life changes such as moving to a new house or a new city, switching jobs, or getting divorced or remarried may seem like proactive, positive steps. But often such major upheavals only compound stress and delay your mourning.

- Keep your life simple right now. Do what you need to do to get through the day. Spend your time with people you love, doing the things that give you pleasure. Eliminate or set limits with friends who drain you or make you feel worse when you're around them.

CARPE DIEM:
Is there a commitment in your life that feels like a burden right now? Maybe you can temporarily give it up. Today, look into de-stressing your schedule.

13.

MAKE AN INVENTORY OF SURVIVAL STRATEGIES.

- What has helped you cope with stress and loss in the past? These strategies will probably help you now, too.

- Make a list of the most difficult times in your life and the ways in which you helped yourself live through them. Did you spend time with family? Turn to your faith? Help take care of someone else? Can you make use any of these survival techniques today?

- Knowing what calms you is also important. Getting a massage, taking a walk, going for a swim, talking to your sister on the phone, walking the dog, reading a book, meditating—find what works for you.

CARPE DIEM:
Make a list of what you need to get through the next month.
Ask your friends and family to help you meet these needs.

14.

LOOK TO THOSE WHO MODEL HOPE AND HEALING.

- As we have said, you are not alone. While no one else feels and grieves exactly as you do over the death of this one special person, many others have experienced similar deaths and learned to live and love fully again.

- You may find it helpful to identify people who have not only survived the sudden, violent death of someone loved, but who have learned to live more deeply as a result.

- Grief support groups may put you in touch with such people. Victim's advocate groups may be another good place to contact. You can also find many good books written by survivors.

- Your place of worship may offer opportunities for you to meet others affected by sudden, violent death. You may want to look into support groups, lay ministries and weekend retreats.

CARPE DIEM:

Whom do you know who—despite adversity—exhibits the kind of love and hopefulness you'd like to regain? Contact this person and ask for his advice over lunch or coffee.

15.

BELIEVE IN YOUR CAPACITY TO HEAL.

- All the veteran traumatized grievers I have ever had the privilege of meeting and learning from would want me to tell you this: You will survive.

- If your loss was recent, you may think you cannot get through this. You can and you will. It will be excruciatingly difficult, yes, but over time and with the love and support of others, your grief will soften and you will find ways to be happy again. There will come a day when the death is not the first thing you think of when you wake up in the morning.

- Many mourners also struggle with feeling they don't *want* to survive. Again, those who have gone before you want you to know that while this feeling is normal, it will pass. One day in the not-too-distant future you will feel that life is worth living again. For now, think of how important you are to your children, your partner, your parents and siblings, your friends.

- As time passes, you may also choose not simply to survive, but to truly live. The remainder of your life can be full and rich and satisfying if you choose life over mere existence.

CARPE DIEM:

If you're feeling you won't make it through the next few weeks or months, talk to someone about your feelings of panic and despair. The simple act of expressing these feelings may render them a little less powerful.

16.

BE PROACTIVE IN YOUR JOURNEY THROUGH GRIEF.

- Our society teaches us that emotional pain is to be avoided, not embraced, yet it is only in moving toward our grief that we can be healed.

- As Helen Keller once said, "The only way to get to the other side is to go through the door." Because of the traumatic nature of this death, you just need to be sure to open the door slowly and only when you are ready. Keep in mind that there are no rewards for speed!

- Being proactive in grief means taking an active role in your healing. One of the most difficult emotions that survivors of sudden, violent death face is the feeling of loss of control. Something awful has happened and you were unable to prevent it. You might feel passive and powerless.

- However, you needn't think of yourself as a powerless victim or as helpless in the face of grief. Instead, empower yourself to "do something" with your grief—to mourn it, to express it outside yourself, to find ways to help yourself heal.

- Be suspicious if you find yourself thinking that you're "doing well" since the death. Sometimes "doing well" means you're avoiding your pain.

CARPE DIEM:

Today, do something to confront and express your grief. Maybe it's time to tell someone close to you how you've really been feeling.

17.

USE LANGUAGE THAT EMPOWERS YOU.

- Sometimes the language we choose affects how we think and feel about our lives. Passive language can make us feel even more victimized. Stronger language can help us regain some sense of control.

- If someone you love died in a drunk driving crash, for example, you may feel more empowered to say that he was "killed" rather than he "died." Using the word "killed" more accurately tells your story and describes that someone's life was taken from you.

- Avoid euphemisms. Saying that someone "passed away" may seem gentler, but does it truly describe the reality and the brutality of what happened? Learn to say the words "death" and "died."

- Similarly, work to find words to describe how you're really feeling. When someone asks, "How are you?", learn to be brief but honest. Say, "I've been feeling really (sad, angry, lonely, etc.)." Or "This week was really hard for me because..." Saying "I'm fine" or "I'm doing OK" may not serve you or the listener well.

CARPE DIEM:
Are there certain words that people use when talking about the death that bother you? The next time you hear them, let the speaker know why his terminology is painful to you.

18.

EMBRACE YOUR SPIRITUALITY.

• Above all, grief is a journey of the soul. It demands you to consider why people live, why people die and what gives life meaning. These are the most spiritual questions we have language to form.

• After a sudden, violent death, most mourners who have faith in God or a higher power end up questioning their beliefs. Can there be a God who would permit such a thing to happen? Why would God be so cruel? And, as Rabbi Harold Kushner asked in his famous book of the same title, Why do bad things happen to good people?

• Rabbi Kushner's own son died of a progressive, fatal disease called progeria. During the course of his son's illness and in the decade that followed, he, a deeply religious man, struggled with his faith and the whys of life and death. He came to believe that God did not cause his son's death and could not have prevented it. Rabbi Kushner came to believe that God, while loving and the source of eternal life, is not all-powerful, that the individual lives of human beings are not always in His control.

• You may want to find books in which other people have shared their struggles with spirituality after a death. From a Christian perspective, some of my favorites are *A Grace Disguised*, by Gerald L. Sittser; *A Grief Observed*, by C.S. Lewis; and *The Will of God*, by Leslie Weatherhead.

• Your faith or spirituality will shift and blur and change as a result of the death. And it may continue to change in the decades to come. Whatever you believe and however your beliefs change, know that your questions, doubts and anger at God do not make you a bad person. You are simply wrestling with what it means to be human.

• Make the effort to embrace your spirituality and it will embrace you back by inspiring you with a sense of peace, hope and healing.

CARPE DIEM:

Perhaps you have a friend who seems spiritually grounded.
Talk to this person about his beliefs and spiritual experiences.
Ask him how he learned to nurture his spirituality.

19.

UNDERSTAND THE SIX NEEDS OF MOURNING

Need #1: Acknowledge the reality of the death.

• You must gently confront the difficult reality that someone you loved is dead and will never physically be present to you again.

• Whether the death was sudden or anticipated, acknowledging the full reality of the loss may occur over weeks and months.

• You will first acknowledge the reality of the loss with your head. Only over time will you come to acknowledge it with your heart. As Stephen Levine has noted, "There are pains that cannot be contained in the mind, only in the heart."

• At times you may push away the reality of the death. This is normal. You will come to integrate the reality in doses as you are ready.

• You may be saying to yourself, "I feel like I'm dreaming. I keep hoping I'll wake up and none of this will have happened." I hear this often from trauma survivors. Your shock protects you from being overwhelmed by the loss. You need and deserve time to reconstitute yourself after this trauma. You need time to become accustomed to thinking and feeling in your new reality. Go slow. There are no rewards for speed.

CARPE DIEM:
Tell someone about the death today. Talking about it will help you work on this important need.

20.

UNDERSTAND THE SIX NEEDS
OF MOURNING

Need #2: Embrace the pain of the loss.

- This need requires mourners to embrace the pain of their loss—something we naturally don't want to do. It is easier to avoid, repress or push away the pain of grief than it is to confront it.

- It is in embracing your grief, however, that you will learn to reconcile yourself to it.

- You will need to slowly—ever so slowly—"dose" yourself in embracing your pain. If you were to allow in all the pain at once, you could not survive.

- People with chronic pain are taught not to tighten around the pain but to relax and allow the pain to be present. When pain is resisted, it intensifies. You don't want to fight with your pain; you want to allow it into your soul in small doses so that eventually you can move from darkness into light.

CARPE DIEM:
If you feel up to it, allow yourself a time for embracing pain today. Dedicate 15 minutes to thinking about and feeling the loss. Reach out to someone who doesn't try to take your pain away and spend some time with him.

21.

UNDERSTAND THE SIX NEEDS OF MOURNING

Need #3: Remember the person who died.

• When someone loved dies, they live on in us through memory.

• To heal, you need to actively remember the person who died and commemorate the life that was lived.

• Never let anyone take your memories away in a misguided attempt to save you from pain. It's good for you to continue to display photos of the person who died. When possible, it's also good for you to stay in the house you shared with the person who died.

• Remembering the past makes hoping for the future possible. As Kierkegaard noted, "Life can only be understood backwards, but it must be lived forwards."

CARPE DIEM:

Brainstorm a list of characteristics or memories of the person who died. Write as fast as you can for 10 minutes (or more), then put away your list for later reflection.

22.

UNDERSTAND THE SIX NEEDS OF MOURNING

Need #4: Develop a new self-identity

• Part of your self-identity was formed by the relationship you had with the person who died.

• You may have gone from being a "wife" to a "widow" or from a "parent" to a "bereaved parent." The way you defined yourself and the way society defines you is changed.

• You need to re-anchor yourself, to reconstruct your self-identity. This is arduous and painful work. One of your biggest challenges may be to recreate yourself in the face of the loss of who you once were. Let me assure you that you can and will do this.

• Many mourners discover that as they work on this need, they ultimately discover some positive changes in their self-identities, such as becoming more caring or less judgmental.

CARPE DIEM:
Write out a response to this prompt: I used to be
_____. Now that _____ died, I am
_____. This makes me feel _____.
Keep writing as long as you want.

23.

UNDERSTAND THE SIX NEEDS OF MOURNING

Need #5: Search for meaning.

• When someone loved dies suddenly and violently, we naturally question the meaning and purpose of life and death.

• "Why?" questions may surface uncontrollably and often precede "How?" questions. "Why did this happen?" comes before "How will I go on living?"

• You will probably question your philosophy of life and explore religious and spiritual values as you work on this need.

• Remember that having faith or spirituality does not negate your need to mourn. "Blessed are those who mourn for they shall be comforted."

• Some people may tell you that asking "Why?" doesn't do you any good. These people are usually unfamiliar with the experience of traumatic grief. Try to reach out to people who can create a supportive atmosphere for you right now.

CARPE DIEM:
Write down a list of "why" questions that have surfaced for you since the death. Find a friend or counselor who will explore these questions with you without thinking she has to give you answers.

24.

UNDERSTAND THE SIX NEEDS OF MOURNING

Need #6: Receive ongoing support from others.

- As mourners, we need the love and understanding of others if we are to heal.

- Don't feel ashamed by your dependence on others right now. Instead, revel in the knowledge that others care about you.

- Unfortunately, our society places too much value on "carrying on" and "doing well" after a death. So, many mourners are abandoned by their friends and family soon after the death.

- One of the touchstones of grief is that each and every one of us as humans are connected by loss. As you experience the physical separation from someone you love, you are connected to every single person who has experienced or ever will experience a similar loss. As The Compassionate Friends (an international organization of bereaved parents) say, "We need not walk alone."

- Grief is a journey, not a destination, and you will need the continued support of your friends and family for weeks, months and years.

CARPE DIEM:
Sometimes your friends want to support you but don't know how. Ask. Call your closest friend right now and tell her you need her help through the coming weeks and months.

25.

KNOW THAT GRIEF DOES NOT PROCEED IN ORDERLY, PREDICTABLE "STAGES."

• Though the "Needs of Mourning" (Ideas 19-24) are numbered 1-6, grief is not an orderly progression towards healing. Don't fall into the trap of thinking your grief journey will be predictable or always forward-moving.

• Usually, grief hurts more before it hurts less.

• I once heard grief compared to Alice's fall into the rabbit hole. One moment Alice is dozing in the garden and the next she is falling into a world where nothing is right. Who is she? Where is she going? Why does nothing make sense? Slowly, over time and after many tribulations, Alice wakes up. But she will never look at things as she did before.

• You will probably experience a multitude of different emotions in a wave-like fashion. You will also likely encounter more than one need of mourning at the same time. Understandably, survivors of sudden, violent death also tend to spend more time and effort on the first need of mourning: acknowledging the reality of the death.

• Be compassionate with yourself as you experience your own unique grief journey.

CARPE DIEM:
Has anyone told you that you are in this or that "stage" of grief? Ignore this usually well-intended advice. Don't allow yourself or anyone else to compartmentalize your grief.

26.

DON'T EXPECT YOURSELF TO MOURN OR HEAL IN A CERTAIN WAY OR IN A CERTAIN TIME.

- Your unique grief journey will be shaped by many factors, including:

  - the nature of the relationship you had with the person who died.
  - the age of the person who died.
  - the circumstances of the death.
  - your unique personality.
  - your cultural background.
  - your religious or spiritual beliefs.
  - your gender.
  - your support systems.

- Because of these and other factors, no two deaths are ever mourned in precisely the same way.

- Don't have rigid expectations for your thoughts, feelings and behaviors. Don't have rigid expectations for the thoughts, feelings and behaviors of others, either. If you have friends or family members who aren't mourning in the ways you think they should be, try to keep in mind that there is no one right way to grieve. Everyone's journey through grief is different.

CARPE DIEM:
Talk to someone else mourning this death—perhaps someone whose mourning style is very different from your own. Compare notes about your grief journeys.

27.

EMBRACE THE UNIQUENESS OF YOUR GRIEF.

- Your grief is what it is. The thoughts and feelings you've been having since the death are what they are. They are neither good nor bad, right nor wrong. They simply are.

- Your grief is unique. There is only one you. And your relationship with the person who died was unique. The circumstances of the death make it unique, too. Go slow.

- I have explained to you the Six Reconciliation Needs of Mourning (Ideas 19-24), for these are the needs that all mourners must undertake to integrate the loss into their heart and soul. But I do not pretend to know all the intricacies of your grief; the Needs of Mourning alone will not define your journey. Besides, they have been naturally complicated by the traumatic nature of the death.

- While mourners often share similar stories and circumstances, no two people grieve in the same way and in the same time. Comparing and judging your grief to another person's separates us on the path we all walk. This is not to say that you can't help each other; survivors of sudden, violent death often understand and empathize with one another in profoundly healing ways. Grief, while as unique as our individual fingerprints, is an experience we all share as human beings.

- Just as you must accept the uniqueness of your own grief, you must also accept the grief responses of others mourning the same death. Others who loved the person who died will grieve in very different ways. Accept these differences and do not judge others for their unique thoughts and feelings.

CARPE DIEM:
Today, talk to someone else grieving this death. Ask her how she's feeling and what she's been thinking about. Share your thoughts and feelings. You may be surprised at both the differences and the similarities in grief.

28.

ACCEPT THAT THERE MAY
BE NO ANSWERS.

• The fourth need of mourning (which I explore in more detail in my book *The Journey Through Grief: Reflections on Healing*) is to search for meaning in life and death. This is the natural process of seeking to understand why such horrible things happen, why people have to die, why you and your family have been affected in this terrible way.

• The search for meaning is a long and painful process, especially after a sudden, violent death. How can one possibly find meaning in this tragedy?

• Many people touched by traumatic loss have come to realize that there may be no meaning to the tragedy itself. No rhyme or reason. No justice. Violent dying is wrong. Period. But they also learn, over time, that there can be meaning in the ways they and others respond to what has happened.

• What will I do now? How can I help prevent this from happening again? In what ways can I honor the life of the person who died? How can I become a more loving, compassionate, helpful person as a result of this tragedy? For many survivors of sudden, violent death, these are ultimately the questions that have answers. These are ultimately the questions that lead to peace and renewed love for life. While you may not be at this place right now in your journey, my hope for you is that peace does indeed come to you.

CARPE DIEM:

Deep in your soul, what is the most troubling question you have about the death? Take a walk today and give yourself some time to consider your question and why it haunts you. When you're ready, you may want to find someone you can trust to explore this question with.

29.

BE AWARE OF "GRIEF OVERLOAD."

- Unfortunately, sometimes people (maybe you) experience more than one loss in a short period of time. A traumatic event may result in many deaths. A child's death may be closely followed by a parent's death. Or an accident will claim the lives of more than one loved one.

- Other types of losses—job changes, divorce, illness, children leaving home—can also occur on top of death loss.

- When this happens, you may be at risk for "grief overload." Your ability to cope may be stretched beyond its limits. You may think of nothing but death. You may feel torn, grieving one death this minute and another death the next. You may feel like you're going crazy.

- Rest assured, you're not going crazy. You are, however, in need of special care. You must try to find ways to cope with all the stress yet still find the time and focus you need to grieve. Reach out to others for help. You cannot get through this alone. See a counselor, if only to help you survive the early weeks after the deaths. Join a support group. Start a grief journal. Be proactive in getting help for yourself and mourning openly. Remember, you have special needs right now and deserve support.

- Fertile soil that produces healthy growth does so because it has been well-tended in the early cycles of the planting season. This is also true with our grief.

CARPE DIEM:

If you're grief overloaded right now, sit down and make a list of five things you can do right now to help offload some of your stress. Make it a point to take action on these five things today.

30.

FIND WAYS TO UNDERSTAND AND COME TO THE LIMITS OF YOUR GUILT.

- I've learned that many survivors of sudden, violent death feel guilty about one thing or another. They feel guilty that they didn't stop their friend from driving that night, that they allowed their child to walk home alone, that they weren't the ones who were killed.

- Understandably, "survivor guilt" is very common among traumatized mourners. You may wonder why it was someone else and not you who died, especially if you were part of the same accident or event. You may wish you could take the place of the person who died so that they might live.

- Talk about any lingering feelings of guilt, regret and remorse. Don't nurse them and continue to punish yourself for them. Your guilt and its attendant feelings of self-doubt, pain and anxiety may block you in your grief journey if you can't find ways to subdue them. Try giving them voice and see how their power over you diminishes.

- Rationally or irrationally, some mourners blame other family members or friends for some aspect of the death. If feelings of blame reside in you, talk compassionately (remember, this person's heart is also broken) to him or her about them.

- I would be remiss if I did not point out that some people are in fact partly or wholly responsible for some deaths, whether intentionally or accidentally. These people often benefit from professional help in dealing with their overwhelming guilt.

CARPE DIEM:
Call a friend who's a good listener or sit down with your partner and say, "I need to tell someone about..." Get any feelings of guilt, remorse and regret off your chest.

31.

CRY.

- Tears are a natural cleansing and healing mechanism. They rid your body of stress chemicals. It's OK to cry. In fact, it's good to cry when you feel like it. What's more, tears are a form of mourning. They are sacred!

- Your pain, your grief, your overwhelming loss disturbs the world around you. Disturb the quiet with your soul's cry.

- On the other hand, don't feel bad if you aren't crying a lot. Not everyone is a crier.

- You may find that those around you are uncomfortable with your tears. As a society, we're often not so good at witnessing others in pain. Don't let those people take your grief away from you.

- Explain to your friends and family that you need to cry right now and that they can help by allowing you to.

- As a trauma survivor, you may even find yourself *keening*, which means a loud wailing or wordless crying out in lament for the dead. Keening is an instinctive form of mourning. It gives voice to your profound pain at a time when words are inadequate.

- You may find yourself crying at unexpected times or places. If you need to, excuse yourself and retreat to somewhere private. Or better yet, go ahead and cry openly and honestly, unashamed of your tears of overwhelming grief.

CARPE DIEM:
If you feel like it, have a good cry today. Find a safe place to embrace your pain and cry as long and as hard as you want to.

32.

BE HONEST WITH THE CHILDREN WHO MOURN.

- Children are often forgotten mourners. We try to protect them from painful realities by not being open and honest with them. We hide our own grief because we don't want them to feel bad.

- But children can cope with what they know. They cannot cope with what they don't know or have never been told. When we're not honest with them, they typically imagine circumstances even worse than the truth of a sudden, violent death.

- Children are amazing, resilient creatures. Tell them the truth. Use language they'll understand, but avoid euphemisms. Don't tell them Daddy went to sleep or God took Daddy. (I've counseled many such children who were secretly counting the days until God would take them, too!) Learn to use the words "death" and "died."

- Typically children require information in "doses." You may not need to explain every detail to them all at once. If you're open and loving with them, they'll come to you with questions as they're ready. Answer these questions honestly. In the long run, it's a mistake to hide even brutal truths.

- Model your own grief for the children in your life. It's OK to let them see you cry and get upset.

- Just as you as an adult have special needs as a trauma survivor, so do children. One of the most loving things you can do for children touched by traumatic death is get them help outside the family. When a family has been affected by traumatic death, you'll often see what I call the "pressure cooker phenomenon." Typically everyone in the family has a high need to feel understood yet a low capacity to be understanding. Because you appropriately need to focus on your own grief right now, you may not be able to help your children. If this is the case, seek help for the children from friends and professional caregivers.

CARPE DIEM:

If a child is mourning this death, get him in to see a good counselor. This will give you some reassurance that you are doing what you can to help the child.

33.

IF YOU WEREN'T ABLE TO SEE THE BODY, FIND OTHER WAYS TO ACKNOWLEDGE THE REALITY OF THE DEATH.

• In cases of violent death, family members are often unable to view the body. Perhaps the body could not be recovered at all. Or maybe it was so altered that medical and law enforcement staff convinced you that you would be more traumatized if you were to see it.

• One problem with never viewing the body is that you may struggle with feelings that the person isn't really dead. After all, the last time you saw her she was alive and healthy. How could she be dead? You may think maybe the person who was buried or cremated wasn't really her (despite that all objective evidence to the contrary) and she'll show up on your doorstep one day soon. Perhaps if the body was never recovered, you may reason, she survived but is suffering from amnesia.

• I often say that our minds can cope with what they know but they cannot cope with what's been kept from them. If you weren't able to view the body, maybe it would help you to read the coroner's report or to have someone read it for you and tell you in layman's terms what the injuries were like. If photos are available and you feel ready, you may want to view them with a trusted friend or family member. Or perhaps you could talk to the doctors, nurses or funeral home staff who cared for the body.

• At the closing ceremony at Ground Zero in New York, an honor guard escorted an empty, flag-draped stretcher out of a huge pit that had been carved from a 10-story pile of wreckage. Tears streamed down the faces of those in attendance as they held photos of the precious family members, friends and co-workers whom they will never touch, see, or hear again. The thirty-minute ceremony was a reminder that only 291 bodies were found intact and that the remains of only 1,102 of the 2,823 killed had been identified.

CARPE DIEM:
Talk to someone you trust. Bring up your thoughts and feelings about never having seen the body. Sometimes simply giving voice to your concerns renders them less powerful.

34.

IF YOU SAW THE BODY AND ITS INJURIES, ALLOW YOURSELF TIME TO CONJURE UP HAPPIER MEMORIES.

- After a sudden, violent death, family members who viewed the body are often glad they did. Many times the injuries are not as disfiguring as they had imagined. And being able to hold and kiss and touch the body one last time helped them acknowledge the reality of the death. Other people chose not to see the body. Trust that you have made the choice that is right for you.

- Still, you may find yourself unable to shake the image of the person's dead body. You may find yourself returning to this photographic memory over and over again. This is normal. In time you will spontaneously recall happier images of the person you loved. If you don't, you may find it helpful to seek the assistance of a compassionate counselor.

- If you actually witnessed the injuries and the death as they were occurring, or if you were the person to find the body, you have special needs that may best be addressed with an experienced trauma or grief counselor. This is not in any way to imply that something is wrong with you, but rather that your experience was so extreme that you may need special help in moving forward in your grief.

CARPE DIEM:
It might help you to spend some time looking at photos of the person who died. Set aside an hour or two to linger over photo albums today. Or better yet, if they're available, watch family videos that include the person who died.

35.

IF YOU'RE AFRAID, FIND WAYS TO FEEL SAFER.

- Fear is a very common emotion for mourners after a sudden, violent death. Our bodies are programmed to feel anxiety and fear in dangerous situations. Our natural "fight or flight" response helps protect us from harm.

- When someone we love has been placed in a dangerous situation and has died as a result, we feel empathy for her. We imagine what it might have been like for her. We imagine what it might be like if the same thing were to happen to us. We imagine what it might be like if someone else close to us were to die.

- For example, I received numerous phone calls from friends and family on 9/11/01 inquiring if I was flying that day. I fly often across North America in my efforts to teach about grief and loss. These calls made me think about my own mortality and how precious life is each day.

- While normal, these thoughts make you feel anxious and unsafe. You may have trouble getting through your day, sleeping, or going out in public.

- You can't begin to mourn and heal until you feel safe. Consider what would make you feel safer right now. Do you need to stay at someone else's house for a while? Would it help you to see a counselor to defuse your overwhelming fears? Would you like some extra help watching over your children?

CARPE DIEM:
If you're feeling afraid—no matter how rational or irrational your fears might seem to you, talk about your fear with someone who makes you feel safe. You might find it helpful to talk to a professional counselor who specializes in trauma loss. Ask for help overcoming your fears.

36.

IF YOU ARE ANGRY, FIND APPROPRIATE WAYS TO EXPRESS YOUR ANGER.

- It's normal to feel intensely angry after a sudden, violent death, especially when someone is at fault for the death. You may obsess over your feelings of rage and hate toward those responsible. In cases of natural disaster or accidental death, you may be mad at God or at the vagaries of fate that led your loved one to be in the wrong place at the wrong time.

- Logically or illogically, you may also feel angry at others around you. You may be angry at your spouse for his response to the death or at your best friend because she has not suffered as you have. It's also common for some mourners to feel angry with the person who died. How could you abandon me! Why did you have to be in that place at that time!

- Anger is normal and necessary. It's our way of protesting a reality we don't like. It helps us survive. It makes good sense that the emotional defense against fear is anger. It makes us feel like we're taking control. It also helps counter more passive, painful feelings of despair and sadness.

- You do have a choice to meet your anger head-on while at the same time gathering as much support as you can from the world around you. If you are angry and end up isolating yourself, you may slide into a chronic depression.

- Like all your feelings, anger is not wrong. It simply is. What you do with your anger can be wrong, however. Never harm yourself or someone else in an attempt to squelch your rage. This will only serve to disempower you.

CARPE DIEM:
Today, do something physical to vent your anger. Go for a fast walk or punch a boxing bag. Smash a tennis ball against a practice wall over and over. Break some dishes—just make sure they aren't your best china (ha-ha).

37.

IF THE DEATH WAS A HOMICIDE, IT'S OK TO FANTASIZE ABOUT HOW YOU WOULD DEAL WITH THE KILLER.

• Revenge fantasies (or what you may have heard referred to as "rage fantasies") are common among the families of homicide victims or other trauma survivors.

• It's OK—and very normal—to think about how you would confront and deal with the person who killed your loved one. Feelings of rage and vengeance are normal and are not "wrong." They simply are.

• Revenge fantasies may give you a feeling of control—something you desperately lack right now. For a time, they may also protect you from encountering the profound feelings of sadness that lie beneath.

• Perhaps you have heard some of the rage-filled thoughts people have had for Osama Bin Laden following 9/11/01. While many were expressed with attempts at humor, there was also a distinct tone of seriousness about them.

• Of course, acting on your revenge fantasies is another matter entirely. Harming someone else would only bring your family more pain. Instead, channel your energies into cooperating with the D.A.'s office to gather evidence to convict the killer. Or volunteer for an organization that helps prevent this type of crime. Or support your government's effort to fight terrorism. Or choose to obsess over ways you could honor the life of the person who died.

CARPE DIEM:
Talk to someone else mourning this death about your revenge fantasies. They probably have similar thoughts and feelings. Sharing these fantasies with each other may be a revealing and healing experience. Again, just be sure not to act them out!

38.

KNOW THAT IT'S OK NOT TO FORGIVE.

- Sudden, violent death often results from the acts of others. Someone may have intentionally murdered the person you loved. Someone may have accidentally killed or contributed to the death of the person you loved.

- The rules of your religion may require you to forgive this person. Or you may simply believe that you should forgive, that you are a lesser or bad person if you are unable to forgive.

- I don't believe that forgiveness is necessary for healing. For some survivors, forgiveness is an important milestone in their journeys through grief; they feel relieved of a heavy burden. For others, heartfelt forgiveness is not to be. If this applies to you, does this mean you're "stuck" in your grief journey or that you'll never truly heal? I don't think so. It simply means you have come to a decision about the morality of the death. This decision, forgiving or unforgiving, is part of your grief.

- In cases of suicide, forgiveness is an even more complex issue. Can you forgive someone you love for taking herself from you? While you may never agree with the act, you may need to make peace with the fact that it happened. In my many years as grief counselor, I have met and spent time with hundreds of suicide survivors. I have found that those who, over time, come to truly forgive are best able to reconnect to life once again.

CARPE DIEM:
If this issue is weighing on your mind, it may help you to talk about what forgiveness or lack of forgiveness means to you. Explore it with a good listener. Express your thoughts and feelings.

39.

BE PROACTIVE AND ASSERTIVE WITH THE CRIMINAL JUSTICE SYSTEM.

- This death may have cast you and your family into the intricacies and vagaries of the criminal justice system. Almost always, sudden and violent deaths require an autopsy and an investigation. In cases of homicide, you may have to endure a lengthy period of investigation and trial.

- It may help you to be assertive in seeking information and follow-up from investigators. Obtain a copy of the crime report and the autopsy. Contact the investigating agency and ask who's in charge of the case. Ask which charges are being considered and why. Ask if there's a victims advocacy program to help you with emotional, legal and financial issues. Ask to be informed as the case moves through hearings, arraignment, trial and sentencing.

- Don't assume that you will be kept informed without asking. Sometimes law enforcement agencies aren't so good at following up with victim's families.

- If you're not feeling up to all this effort, ask a friend of the family to be your liaison with the criminal justice system and to bring you pertinent news.

CARPE DIEM:
If you have any unresolved questions or issues with the criminal justice system regarding your loved one's death, call today and track down the answers you've been worrying over.

40.

IF THIS DEATH HAS PUT YOUR FAMILY IN THE MEDIA SPOTLIGHT, APPOINT SOMEONE TO HANDLE MEDIA INQUIRIES FOR YOU.

- Often sudden and violent deaths are front page news. Over and over you may hear about the death on TV, on the radio or in your newspaper. This phenomenon tends to make families feel a strange sense of disjointedness, as if the death that they personally experienced also happened on another, more abstract plane.

- The public realm may have laid claim to this death, but it is still first and foremost your personal loss. Focus on your family's grief. Focus on your own physical, emotional, social and spiritual wellbeing. Do what feels right for you.

- Some families find that in being open with the media, they are able to share their personal stories in a way that helps both them and the community mourn. Others find that to mourn and heal, they must withdraw and grieve more privately among close family and friends. I trust that you will do what is right for you and your family.

- Be assertive with media representatives. Tell them what your limits are in terms of talking about the death. Ask not to be contacted or to be contacted through an attorney or specially appointed advocate. If you clearly spell out your preferred boundaries, most people in the media will respect them. If they don't, you might need to consult legal authorities regarding your rights.

CARPE DIEM:
If you are still receiving media inquiries about the death, appoint someone to handle them. This could be a family member, a friend of the family, or an attorney.

41.

GET HELP WITH FINANCIAL STRESSES.

- Death often causes financial difficulties on top of the emotional and spiritual stresses. Emergency medical care and funerals can be very expensive. Lost work time, attorney's fees, and travel costs can all contribute to financial overload.

- If you or your family is under financial stress right now, ask for help. Ask someone you trust to take charge of your finances right now so you can concentrate on your grief. Call your consumer credit counseling agency. Consolidate your debts with a home equity loan. Your local Victim's Advocate Fund may also be able to make a contribution.

- Whatever you do, don't ignore your finances right now. Delinquencies and defaulting on loans will only cause you bigger headaches in the months to come.

CARPE DIEM:
Among your friends and family, who's the best financial manager you know? Ask this person to step in and help you with money issues for the next several months.

42.

REACH OUT AND TOUCH.

- For many people, physical contact with another human being is healing. It has been recognized since ancient times as having transformative, healing powers.

- Have you hugged anyone lately? Held someone's hand? Put your arm around another human being?

- You probably know several people who enjoy hugging or physical touching. If you're comfortable with their touch, encourage it in the weeks and months to come.

- Hug someone you feel safe with. Kiss your children or a friend's baby. Walk arm in arm with a neighbor.

- You may want to listen to the song titled "I Know What Love Is," by Don White. I have found this song helps me reflect on the power of touch. Listen to this song then drop me a note or e-mail (wolfelt@centerforloss.com) and let me know how it makes you think, and more important, feel.

CARPE DIEM:

Try hugging your close friends and family members today, even if you usually don't. You just might like it!

43.

USE THE NAME OF THE PERSON WHO DIED.

- When you're talking about the death or about your life in general, don't avoid using the name of the person who died. Using the name lets others know they can use it, too.

- Acknowledge the significance of the death by talking about the person who died: "I remember when Jesse . . .", "I was thinking of Sarah today because . . ."

- Encourage your friends and family to use the name of the person who died, too. I know I love to hear the names of the people in my life who have died. How about you?

CARPE DIEM:
Flip through a baby name book at a local bookstore or library and look up the name of the person who died. Reflect on the name's meaning as it relates to the unique person you loved.

44.

WRITE A LETTER.

- Sometimes articulating our thoughts and feelings in letter-form helps us understand them better.

- Write a letter to the person who died telling her how you feel now that she's gone. Consider the following prompts:

  - What I miss most about you is . . .
  - What I wish I'd said or hadn't said is . . .
  - What's hardest for me now is . . .
  - What I'd like to ask you is . . .
  - I'm keeping my memories of you alive by . . .

- Read your letter aloud at the cemetery.

- Another healing exercise can be writing a letter to yourself on behalf of the person who died. Imagine that the person who died is writing you from heaven. What would she say to you? How would she want you to live the rest of your life?

- Write a letter to God telling him how you feel about the death.

- Write thank you notes to helpers such as hospice staff, neighbors, doctors, funeral directors, etc.

CARPE DIEM:
Write a letter to someone you love who's still alive telling her why she's so important to you.

45.

SEEK SUPPORT ON ANNIVERSARIES.

- Anniversaries—of the death, life events, birthdays—can be especially hard when you are in grief.

- In cases of sudden, violent death, the anniversary of the death is usually very painful. Thoughts about how the person died resurface. Anger at those responsible boils again. Fear and anxiety often heighten.

- These are times you may want to plan ahead for. The anniversary of the death may be a good day to plan a small memorial service at the site of the death or the cemetery or scattering site. Ritualizing your thoughts and feelings through prayer, song and memory-sharing with others will help create positive, healing structure on this day.

- Reach out to others on birthdays and other anniversaries. Talk about your feelings with a close friend.

CARPE DIEM:
What's the next anniversary you've been anticipating?
Make a plan right now for what you will do on that day.
Enlist a friend's help so you won't be alone.

46.

UNDERSTAND THE ROLE OF "LINKING OBJECTS."

• You may be comforted by physical objects associated with the person who died. You may save clothing, jewelry, toys, locks of hair and other personal items.

• Such "linking objects" may help you remember the person who died and honor the life that was lived. Such objects may help you heal.

• Never think that being attached to these objects is morbid or wrong.

• Never hurry into disposing of the personal effects of the person who died. You may want to leave personal items untouched for months or sometimes years. This is OK as long as the objects offer comfort and don't inhibit healing.

• Watch out for people who try to tell you that if you force yourself to get rid of linking objects, it will help you "accept" the loss. These people may be well-intentioned but are sadly misinformed.

CARPE DIEM:

When and only when you're ready, ask a friend or family member to help you sort through the personal belongings of the person who died. Fill a memory box with significant objects and mementos.

47.

IF YOU HAVE DREAMS OF THE PERSON WHO DIED, SHARE THEM WITH SOMEONE CLOSE TO YOU.

- Mourners often dream about the person who died. This is a normal response to loss and grief.

- After a sudden, violent death, you may have dreams that are upsetting, even violent. You may dream about the circumstances of the death. You may dream that you are there when the death occurs (but still helpless to prevent it). You may have seemingly unrelated nightmares. These dreams are your mind's way of attempting to process the reality of the death.

- If you are consistently having nightmares following the death, I strongly suggest you see a professional counselor. You deserve to get help to understand what you might be able to do to help yourself convert your nightmares into dreams.

- On the other hand, you may have very happy, reassuring dreams about the person who died. You may even feel you have been "visited" by him in your dreams. Perhaps he has told you that he's OK and that you'll be OK, too.

- It's also normal NOT to dream about the death or the person who died. You may be sleeping poorly and thus not dreaming in your normal pattern. Or you may be having dreams but not remembering them.

CARPE DIEM:
Talking about your dreams—whether they're happy or sad—is another way to express your grief. Or you might consider starting a "dream journal" in which you record your dreams as soon as you wake up.

48.

KEEP A JOURNAL.

- Journals are an ideal way for some mourners to record thoughts and feelings.

- Remember—your inner thoughts and feelings of grief need to be expressed outwardly (which includes writing) if you are to heal.

- Consider jotting down your thoughts and feelings first thing when you wake up or each night before you go to sleep. Your journal entries can be as long or as short as you want.

- Don't worry about what you're writing or how well you're writing it. Just write whatever comes into your mind. To get started, set a timer for five or ten minutes and write as much as you can without stopping.

- After a sudden, violent death, it can feel like you're stuck in your grief. Keeping a journal allows you to look back at entries from last month or last year and see the progress you've made.

CARPE DIEM:
Stop by your local bookstore and choose a blank book you like the look and feel of. Visit a park on your way home, find a quiet bench and write your first entry.

49.

ORGANIZE A TREE PLANTING.

- Trees represent the beauty, vibrancy and continuity of life.

- A specially planted and located tree can honor the person who died and serves as a perennial memorial. This can be particularly helpful if no body was recovered. The tree is a symbolic, physical presence that helps represent the person who died. When you visit the tree, it helps you remember the person who died and convert your grief into mourning.

- You might write a short ceremony for the tree planting. (Or ask a friend to write one.) Consider a personalized metal marker or sign, too.

- For a more private option, plant a tree in your own yard. Consult your local nursery for an appropriate selection. Flowering trees are especially beautiful in the spring.

CARPE DIEM:
Order a tree for your own yard and plant it in honor of the person who died. You'll probably need someone to help you prepare the hole and place the tree.

50.

PLAN A CEREMONY.

- When words are inadequate, have ceremony.

- Ceremony assists in reality, recall, support, expression, transcendence.

- When personalized, the funeral ceremony can be a healing ritual.
  But ceremonies that take place later on can also be very meaningful.
  For example, a number of ceremonies have taken place at the site of
  the World Trade Center and ceremonies will likely continue to be held
  there on the anniversaries of the tragedy. Ongoing ritual helps you
  continue to both remember and integrate the loss into your head,
  heart and soul.

- The ceremony might center on memories of the person who died,
  "meaning of life" thoughts and feelings or affirmation of faith.

- In the Jewish body of faith there is a practice called Yizkor, the
  "remembering" prayer. Anyone in the synagogue who is not saying
  Yizkor is asked to leave until the prayer is completed. This ritual of
  having people leave is intended to protect the intimacy and sanctity
  of the sacred space for those who mourn.

CARPE DIEM:

Hold a candle-lighting memory ceremony. Invite a small group of
friends. Form a circle around a center candle, with each person holding
their own small candle. Have each person light their memory candle
and share a memory of the person who died. At the end, play a song or
read a poem or prayer in memory of the person who died.

51.

ORGANIZE A MEMORY BOOK.

• Assembling a scrapbook that holds treasured photos and mementos of the person who died can be a very helpful activity.

• You might consider including a birth certificate, schoolwork, newspaper clippings, locks of hair, old letters.

• Phone others who loved the person who died and ask them to write a note or contribute photos.

• Other ideas: a memory box, photo buttons of the person who died (nice for a child or younger person), a memory quilt.

CARPE DIEM:

Buy an appropriate scrapbook or keepsake box today. Don't forget to buy the associated materials you'll need, such as photo pages or photo corners, glue, scissors, etc.

52.

DON'T BE CAUGHT OFF GUARD BY "GRIEFBURSTS."

- Sometimes heightened periods of sadness may overwhelm you. These times can seem to come of out nowhere and can be frightening and painful.

- Even long after the death, something as simple as a sound, a smell or a phrase can bring on a "griefburst." You may see someone in a crowd who resembles the person who died. You may come across an old jacket or tennis racquet that belonged to the person who died. You may smell a certain food or cologne that reminds you of the person who died. These experiences tend to trigger sudden, unexpected and powerful waves of emotion.

- I often think that griefbursts are the way the person who has died says to you, "Don't forget me. Please don't forget me."

- Allow yourself to experience griefbursts without shame or self-judgment, no matter where and when they occur. If you would feel more comfortable, retreat to somewhere private when these strong feelings surface.

CARPE DIEM:
Create an action plan for your next griefburst. For example, you might plan to drop whatever you are doing and go for a walk or record thoughts in your journal.

53.

PRAY.

- Prayer is mourning because prayer means taking your feelings and articulating them to someone else. Even when you pray silently, you're forming words for your thoughts and feelings and you're offering up those words to a presence outside yourself.

- Someone wise once noted, "Our faith is capable of reaching the realm of mystery."

- Did you know that real medical studies have shown that prayer can actually help people heal?

- If you believe in a higher power, pray. Pray for the person who died. Pray for your questions about life and death to be answered. Pray for the strength to embrace your pain and to go on to find continued meaning in life and living. Pray for others affected by this death.

- Many places of worship have prayer lists. Call yours and ask that your name be added to the prayer list. On worship days, the whole congregation will pray for you. Often many individuals will pray at home for those on the prayer list, as well.

CARPE DIEM:

Bow your head right now and say a silent prayer. If you are out of practice, don't worry; just let your thoughts flow naturally.

54.

LEARN SOMETHING NEW.

- Sometimes mourners feel stuck. We can feel depressed and the daily routine of our lives can seem joyless.

- Perhaps you would enjoy learning something new or trying a new hobby. When you direct your mind through learning, you can feel some sense of control of your life. The trauma you are experiencing has ripped away your sense of control. Regain a little piece of it by learning something new.

- What have you always wanted to learn but have never tried? Playing the guitar? Woodworking? Speaking French?

- Consider physical activities. Learning to play golf or doing karate have the added benefits of exercise.

CARPE DIEM:
Get ahold of your local community calendar and sign up for a class in something you haven never tried before.

55.

BE A KID AGAIN.

- Sometimes we all just need to go back to a time when we were kids, when we were innocent and carefree, before loss touched our lives.

- You can do it. How long has it been since you went wading in a stream or running through the sprinkler? How about jumping in a pile of dried leaves? Or shuffling barefoot across freshly-mown grass? When's the last time you built a sandcastle?

- It is the nature of children to live for the moment and appreciate today. All of us would benefit from a little more childlike wonder.

- Do something childish—blow bubbles, skip rope, visit a toy store, fly a kite, climb a tree.

- If kids aren't already a part of your life, make arrangements to spend some time with them. Volunteer at a local school. Take a friend's children to the park one afternoon.

CARPE DIEM:
Right now, leave your inhibitions behind. Go do one of your favorite childhood activities. You deserve this "time-out" from your overwhelming grief.

56.

PICTURE THIS.

- The visual arts have a way of making us see the world anew.

- Perhaps you would enjoy a visit to an art gallery or museum, a sculpture garden, a photography exhibit.

- Why not try to create some art yourself? Attend a watercolor or calligraphy class.

- Making pottery is something almost everyone enjoys. It's tactile and messy and whimsical.

- I used to love to fingerpaint. No one has ever paid money for one of my originals, but what the heck—they are my best work in the realm of art. Be the best artist you can be.

CARPE DIEM:
Buy some paints, some brushes and a canvas and paint your feelings about the death. Don't worry about your artistic abilities; just let your imagination take charge.

57.

VOLUNTEER.

• Consider honoring the life and the death through social activism. If the person who died was a victim of drunk driving, participate in a local MADD rally. If a loved one completed suicide, volunteer for your local suicide hotline.

• Volunteer at a senior center, an elementary school, a local hospital—someplace befitting the person who died.

• My friends Bonnie and Tony Redfern have started an annual run in their community of Fresno, California, in loving memory of their son Scott, who died suddenly in a tragic shop accident at school. Another couple I am close to, Nancy and Gary Zastrow, founded educational programs, support groups and a newsletter in their town of Wausau, Wisconsin following the suicide death of their beloved son, Chad. And my treasured friend Andrea Gambill started *Bereavement* Magazine after an auto accident took the life of her darling daughter, Judy. All of these special people have helped countless others as a way to honor life and make sense of death.

• If your schedule is too hectic, offer money instead of time. Make your donation in memory of the person who died.

CARPE DIEM:
Call your local United Way and ask for some suggestions about upcoming events you could participate in.

58.

LAUGH.

- Humor is one of the most healing gifts of humanity. Laughter restores hope and assists us in surviving the pain of grief.

- Don't fall into the trap of thinking that laughing and having fun are somehow a betrayal of the person who died. Laughing doesn't mean you don't miss the person who died. Laughing doesn't mean you aren't in mourning.

- Sometimes it helps to think about what the person who died would want for you. Wouldn't she want you to laugh and continue to find joy in life, even in the midst of your sorrow?

- You can only embrace the pain of your loss a little at a time, in doses. In between the doses, it's perfectly normal, even necessary, to love and laugh.

- Remember the fun times you shared with the person who died. Remember his sense of humor. Remember his grin and the sound of his laughter.

- I've heard it said that laughter is a form of internal jogging. Not only is it enjoyable, it is good for you. Studies show that smiling, laughing and feeling good enhance your immune system and make you healthier. If you act happy, you may even begin to feel some happiness in your life again.

CARPE DIEM:

Close your eyes right now and try to remember the smile and the laughter of the person who died. Over time, encouraging yourself to remember the good times will help you focus less on thoughts of the death itself.

59.

VISIT THE GREAT OUTDOORS.

- For many people it is restorative and energizing to spend time outside.

- You may find nature's timeless beauty healing. The sound of a bird singing or the awesome presence of an old tree can help put things in perspective. Mother Earth knows more about kicking back than all the stress management experts on the planet—and she charges far less.

- Go on a nature walk. Or camping. Or canoeing. The farther away from civilization the better.

- I remember a recent time when I was feeling overwhelmed and I just went for a walk. I saw beautiful flowers. I saw leaves falling from the trees. I watched my Husky dogs leap with joy. I took long, deep breaths. I felt a sense of gratitude. After the walk, I felt renewed, changed.

CARPE DIEM:
Call your area forest service for a map of nearby walking or hiking trails. Take a hike sometime this week.

60.

SURF THE WEB.

- The World Wide Web has a number of interesting and informative resources for mourners.

- Many articles about grief are available online. Books can also be purchased online. Most grief organizations (MADD, Parents of Murdered Children, American Association of Suicidology, Widowed Persons Service) now have Web pages.

- Search the word "grief" and see what you find. Use a more specific term (widow, homicide, etc.) if appropriate.

- Like face-to-face support groups, internet chat groups can be healing for some mourners.

CARPE DIEM:

Sit down at your computer today and do a search. If you don't own a computer or have access to one at work, visit your local library. Don't forget to visit the Center for Loss Website: www.centerforloss.com. We want to hear from you about where you are in your grief journey—today, right now. I'll even answer your e-mail (though I'm about six weeks behind...).

61.

FIND A GRIEF "BUDDY."

- Though no one else will grieve this death just like you, there are often others who have had similar experiences.

- Find a grief "buddy"—someone who is also mourning a sudden, violent death, someone you can talk to, someone who also needs a companion in grief right now.

- Make a pact with your grief buddy to call each other whenever one of you needs to talk. Promise to listen without judgment. Commit to spending time together.

- You might arrange to meet once a week for breakfast or lunch with your grief buddy.

- Perhaps you've heard it said, "Friends are not a luxury, they are a necessity." This could never be more of a truth for you than right now.

CARPE DIEM:
Do you know someone who also needs grief support right now? Call her and ask her out to lunch today. If it feels right, discuss the possibility of being grief buddies.

62.

THINK POSITIVE.

- After a traumatic death, it's normal—even necessary—to feel numb, depressed, afraid, angry and many other difficult feelings. You may well be worried about your safety or the safety of others you love. The world has become a scary place and someone you love has been taken from you.

- Indeed, you must allow yourself ample time to acknowledge and experience your painful thoughts and feelings. Life will be hard for a while.

- But over time and with the love and support of others, your life can be happy again. You must trust in your ability to heal. You must trust that you will live and love fully again.

- Even in the midst of your grief, strive to think positive. Neuroscientists now understand that the human brain has the power to create its own reality. If you believe—really believe—that you can do something, you probably can.

- Visualize yourself nurturing a friendship or achieving a goal. Visualize yourself laughing and having fun. Visualize yourself at peace. You may not be able to live these realities today, but projecting yourself forward into a happier future may well help you achieve that future.

CARPE DIEM:

The death is in the past. You cannot change that, but you can affect the future. What is most worrying you about the coming days or weeks? Close your eyes and visualize a positive outcome to the situation.

63.

WATCH FOR WARNING SIGNS.

- Sometimes mourners fall back on self-destructive behaviors to get through this difficult time.

- Try to be honest with yourself about drug or alcohol abuse. Long after the death, are you still taking drugs—prescription or otherwise—to make it through the day? Are you drinking in an attempt to dull the pain? If you're in over your head, ask someone for help.

- Keep in mind that trauma can actually change the biochemistry of the brain. You may very appropriately be taking some anti-depressant, anti-anxiety or sleeping medications right now. And if you were taking medications before the trauma, you should continue doing so under your doctor's supervision. If you're forgetting to take your medication, ask someone to help you remember.

- Are you having suicidal thoughts and feelings? Are you isolating yourself too much? Talk to someone today.

CARPE DIEM:
Acknowledging to ourselves that we have a problem
may come too late. If someone suggests that you need help,
consider yourself lucky to be so well-loved and get help.

64.

BRIGHTEN UP YOUR ENVIRONMENT.

- Would your home or office benefit from a little sprucing up?

- Paint your living room or office in a fresh, new color. Paint is inexpensive and easy to redo.

- Sometimes something as minor as new valances and freshly cleaned windowpanes can make a big difference.

- Pull back the curtains, open the shades and let the sun shine in. Sunlight increases your body's serotonin levels and buoys your mood.

CARPE DIEM:
Select one little project that will help make your environment more pleasant or more soothing. Ask a friend to help you complete the project this weekend.

65.

TELL SOMEONE YOU LOVE THEM.

- Your tragic loss has you very aware of how love makes the world go 'round.

- Sometimes we love people so much, we forget to tell them "I love you." Or we (mistakenly) believe that they know they are loved, so we don't need to tell them.

- These three simple words have deep, spiritual meaning, yet we sometimes fail to see that until it's too late.

- My dad loved me, but it wasn't until just before his death that he whispered to me, "I love you." I miss you, Dad.

CARPE DIEM:
Call someone you love right now and give them the lasting
gift of telling them you love them.

66.

SIMPLIFY YOUR LIFE.

- Many of us today are taking stock of what's really important in our lives and trying to discard the rest.

- You may feel overwhelmed by all the tasks and commitments you have. If you can rid yourself of some of those extraneous burdens, you'll have more time for mourning and healing.

- What is it that is overburdening you right now? Have your name taken off junk mail lists, ignore your dirty house, stop attending any optional meetings you don't look forward to.

CARPE DIEM:
Cancel your newspaper subscription(s) if you're depressed by what you read. Quit watching TV news for a while.

67.

ESTABLISH A MEMORIAL FUND IN THE NAME OF THE PERSON WHO DIED.

- Sometimes bereaved families ask that memorial contributions be made to specified charities in the name of the person who died. This practice allows friends and family members to show their support while helping the family feel that something good came of the death.

- You can establish a personalized and ongoing memorial to the person who died.

- What was meaningful to the person who died? Did she support a certain nonprofit or participate in a certain recreational activity? Was she politically active? Is there an organization that tries to prevent the kind of death she suffered?

- Your local bank or funeral home may have ideas about how to go about setting up a memorial fund.

CARPE DIEM:

Call another friend of the person who died and together brainstorm a list of ideas for a memorial. Suggest that both of you commit to making at least one additional phone call for information before the day is out.

68.

LOOK INTO SUPPORT GROUPS.

• Grief support groups are a healing, safe place for many mourners to express their thoughts and feelings.

• Support groups help mourners know that they're not alone. Members both support one another and learn from each other. And support groups often develop into very tight-knit, loyal and lasting social circles.

• Sharing similar experiences with other mourners may help you feel like you're not alone, that you're not going crazy.

• Your local funeral home or hospice may offer a free or low-cost support group.

• If you are newly bereaved, you may not feel ready for a support group. Many mourners are more open to joining a support group 6-9 months after the death.

• *Bereavement* Magazine keeps an updated list of support groups throughout North America. Contact them at bereavementmag.com.

CARPE DIEM:
Call around today for support group information. If you're feeling ready, plan to attend a meeting this week or next.

69.

PREPARE YOURSELF FOR THE HOLIDAYS.

• Because the person who died is no longer there to share the holidays with, you may feel particularly sad and vulnerable during Christmas, Hanukkah and other holidays.

• Don't overextend yourself during the holidays. Don't feel you have to shop, bake, entertain, send cards, etc. if you're not up for it.

• Sometimes old holiday rituals are comforting after a death and sometimes they're not. Continue them only if they feel good to you; consider creating new ones, as well.

• Take inventory of who you want to spend holiday time with and who you don't. I always use my "Theory of Thirds": one-third of the people in your life will neither help nor hinder you in your grief; one-third will make you feel worse for simply having been around them; and the remaining third will help you feel supported and loved. Try to seek out the latter third and limit contact with the other two-thirds.

CARPE DIEM:

What's the next major holiday? Make a game plan right now and let those you usually spend the day with know of your plan well in advance.

70.

IGNORE HURTFUL ADVICE.

- Sometimes well-intended but misinformed friends will hurt you unknowingly with their words.

- You may be told:

  - I know how you feel.
  - Get on with your life.
  - Keep your chin up.
  - It was God's will.
  - Be glad it was quick.
  - Think of all you have to be thankful for.
  - Now you have an angel in heaven.
  - Time heals all wounds.
  - You're strong. You'll get through this.

- Don't take this advice to heart. Such clichés are often offered because people don't know what else to say. The problem is, phrases like these diminish your unique and significant loss.

CARPE DIEM:
Before your loss, did you ever offer some of these very same phrases to others touched by grief? Most of us have. Learn to forgive these all-too-human mistakes.

71.

MAKE A LIST OF GOALS.

- While you should not set a particular time and course for your healing, it may help you to have made other life goals for the coming year.

- Make a list of short-term goals for the next three months. Perhaps some of the goals could have to do with mourning activities (e.g. make a memory book).

- Also make a list of long-term goals for the next year. Be both realistic and compassionate with yourself as you consider what's feasible and feels good and what will only add too much stress to your life.

CARPE DIEM:

Write a list of goals for this week. Your goals may be as simple as: Go to work every day. Tell John I love him once a day. Take a walk on Tuesday night.

72.

DO SOMETHING YOU'RE GOOD AT.

- Often it helps mourners to find ways to affirm their worth to others and to themselves.

- Do something you're good at! Ride a bike. Bake a cake. Do the crossword puzzle. Write a poem. Play with your kids. Talk to a friend.

- Have other people told you you're good at this or that? Next time you're complimented in this way, take it to heart.

- Recognize your unique talents and gifts. Start each day acknowledging how unique you are!

CARPE DIEM:

Make a list of ten things you're good at. Post it where you can see it every morning. Do one of them today and afterwards, reflect on how you feel.

73.

REACH OUT TO OTHERS FOR HELP.

- Perhaps the most compassionate thing you can do for yourself at this difficult time is to reach out for help from others.

- Think of it this way: Grieving may be the hardest work you have ever done. And hard work is less burdensome when others lend a hand. Life's greatest challenges—getting through school, raising children, pursuing a career—are in many ways team efforts. So it should be with mourning.

- Sharing your pain with others won't make it disappear, but it will, over time, make it more bearable.

- Reaching out for help also connects you to other people and strengthens the bonds of love that make life seem worth living again. But just like gardens, good friends must be cultivated. True friends are blessings during overwhelming times such as this. If you have some, give thanks!

- When Bill Cosby's son Ennis was murdered, Mr. Cosby reached out to other families who were that day also confronted with the murder of their children. He was not alone and you aren't either.

CARPE DIEM:
Call a close friend who may have distanced himself from you since the death and tell him how much you need him right now. Suggest specific ways he can help.

74.

PRACTICE BREATHING IN AND OUT.

- Sometimes what we need most is just to "be." In our goal-oriented society, many of us have lost the knack for simply living.

- Drop all your plans and obligations for today and do nothing.

- Meditate if meditation helps center you. Find someplace quiet, be still, close your eyes and focus on breathing in and out. Relax your muscles. Listen to your own heartbeat.

- Breathing opens you up. Trauma may have closed you down. The power of breath helps to fill your empty spaces. The old wisdom of "count to ten" is all about taking a breath to open up space for something else to happen.

- Consciously breathe in and out; you can slow the world down and touch the edges of your true self.

CARPE DIEM:
Sit down, focus on something 20 feet away and take 10 deep breaths.

75.

TALK OUT LOUD TO THE PERSON WHO DIED.

• Sometimes it feels good to talk to the person who died. Pretend he's sitting in the chair across from you and tell him how you're doing.

• Talk to photos of the person who died. Share your deepest thoughts and feelings with her. Make it part of your daily routine to say "Good morning!" to that photo on your nightstand. (Just be careful who's in earshot!)

• Visit the cemetery, the columbarium or scattering place if the person was cremated or the place that the person died, and if you're not too self-conscious, talk to the person you loved so much.

CARPE DIEM:
If you haven't already, put a photo of the person who died in your wallet or purse. Make it a habit to look at the photo and tell the person what's going on in your life that day.

76.

TALK TO A COUNSELOR.

- While grief counseling is not for everyone, many mourners are helped through their grief journeys by a compassionate counselor. Survivors of sudden, violent death may be helped through post-traumatic distress issues, especially.

- If possible, find a counselor who has experience with grief and loss. A counselor experienced with trauma loss and PTSD is even better.

- Ask your friends for referrals to a counselor they've been helped by. Be a shopper.

- Your church pastor may also be a good person to talk to during this time, but only if she affirms your need to mourn this death and search for meaning.

- Depending on who died and the exact nature of the death, your family may benefit from family counseling sessions. Sometimes this is the only way to share difficult stories and hear one another talk about painful thoughts and feelings.

CARPE DIEM:
Schedule an initial interview with at least two counselors so you can see whom you're most comfortable with.

77.

SAY NO.

- Especially soon after the death, you may lack the energy as well as the desire to participate in activities you used to find pleasurable.

- It's OK to say no when you're asked to help with a project or attend a party. Write a note to the people who've invited you and explain your feelings. Be sure to thank them for the invitation.

- You may have never learned to say no, but now you must. Perhaps you've seen the wonderful sign that says, "What part of NO do you not understand?" You need to learn how to say no to extra projects and social events and invitations that you don't have time or energy for. If anyone needs some quiet time right now, it's you!

- Realize that you can't keep saying no forever. There will always be that first wedding, christening, birthday party, etc. Don't miss out on life's most joyful celebrations.

CARPE DIEM:
Say no to something today. Allow yourself not to feel guilty about it.

78.

TAKE A MINI-VACATION.

- Don't have time to take time off? Plan several mini-vacations this month instead.

- What creative ideas can you come up with to renew yourself? Here are a few ideas to get you started.

  - Schedule a massage with a professional massage therapist.
  - Have a spiritual growth weekend. Retreat into nature. Plan some alone time.
  - Go for a drive with no particular destination in mind. Explore the countryside, slow down and observe what you see.
  - Treat yourself to a night in a hotel or bed and breakfast.
  - Visit a museum or a zoo.
  - Go to a yard sale or auction.
  - Go rollerskating or rollerblading with a friend.
  - Drop by a health food store and walk the aisles.

- Remember—you can have fun and grieve at the same time. Don't feel guilty for needing a break; it will help you survive and revive.

CARPE DIEM:
Plan a mini-vacation for today. Spend one hour
doing something renewing.

79.

RECONNECT WITH SOMEONE SPECIAL.

- Throughout our lives, we often lose contact with people who've touched us or made a difference somehow.

- Death can make us realize that keeping in touch with these people is well worth the effort.

- Whom have you loved or admired but haven't spoken with for a long time?

- For example: teachers, old lovers, childhood friends, past neighbors, former colleagues.

CARPE DIEM:
Write a letter to someone you haven't been in touch with
for a long time. Track down her address and phone number.
Catch her up on your life and invite her to do the same by
calling you or writing you back.

80.

REMEMBER OTHERS WHO HAD A SPECIAL RELATIONSHIP WITH THE PERSON WHO DIED.

• At times your appropriately inward focus will make you feel alone in your grief. You may only be able to focus on you and your own feelings for some time. This is normal and necessary.

• Later, when you are ready, try to think about others who were affected by this death: friends, lovers, teachers, neighbors.

• Is there someone outside of the accepted "circle of mourners" who may be struggling with this death? Perhaps you could call her and offer your condolences.

CARPE DIEM:
Today, write and mail a brief supportive note to someone else affected by the death.

81.

DESIGNATE A TIME TO MOURN EACH DAY.

- Consider making mourning part of your daily routine, just like taking a shower or reading the newspaper.

- Set aside a quiet time each day for embracing your thoughts and feelings about the death.

- The first 20 minutes after you wake up might work. This also might be a good time to journal your thoughts and feelings.

- Sometimes creating a dedicated mourning time allows you to concentrate on living the rest of your day.

CARPE DIEM:
Schedule a "mourning time" for tomorrow.
Write it down in your daily planner.

82.

SCHEDULE SOMETHING THAT GIVES YOU PLEASURE EACH AND EVERY DAY.

- When we're in mourning, often we need something to look forward to, a reason to get out of bed today.

- It's hard to look forward to each day when you know you will be experiencing pain and sadness.

- To counterbalance your normal and necessary mourning, plan something you enjoy doing every day.

- Reading, baking, going for a walk, having lunch with a friend, playing computer games—whatever brings you enjoyment. (Just remember—no inappropriate risk-taking.)

CARPE DIEM:
What's on tap for today? Squeeze in something you enjoy, no matter how hectic your schedule.

83.

IDENTIFY THREE PEOPLE YOU CAN TURN TO ANYTIME YOU NEED A FRIEND.

- You may have many people who care about you but few who are able to be good companions in grief.

- Identify three people whom you think can be there for you in the coming weeks and months.

- Don't assume that others will help. Even normally compassionate people sometimes find it hard to be present to others in grief, especially in cases of sudden, violent death.

CARPE DIEM:
Call these three people and ask them outright: Will you please help me with my grief? Tell them you mainly need to spend time with them and to be able to talk to them freely.

84.

SPEND TIME ALONE.

- Reaching out to others while we're in mourning is necessary. Mourning is hard work and you can't get through it by yourself.

- Still, you will also need alone time to gently work on the six needs of mourning. To slow down and to turn inward, you must sometimes insist on solitude.

- As the famous Swiss psychiatrist Carl Jung wrote, "When you are up against a wall, be still and put down roots, until clarity comes from deeper sources to see over the wall."

- Schedule alone time into each week. Go for a walk in the woods. Lock your bedroom door and read a book. Work in your garden.

- Don't shut your friends and family out altogether, but do heed the call for contemplative silence.

CARPE DIEM:
Schedule one hour of solitude into your day today.

85.

TURN TO YOUR FAMILY.

- In today's mobile, disconnected society, many people have lost touch with the gift of family. Your friends may come and go, but family, as they say, is forever.

- If you're emotionally close to members of your family, you're probably already reaching out to them for support. Allow them to be there for you. Let them in.

- If you're not emotionally close to your family, perhaps now is the time to open closed doors. Call a family member you haven't spoken to for a while. Hop in a car or on a plane and make a long overdue visit.

- Don't feel bad if you have to be the initiator; instead, expend your energy by writing that first letter or making that first phone call.

- On the other hand, you probably know some family members you should keep your distance from. They may be among the one-third who are bound to make you feel worse (see Idea 69). Remember, sometimes you can love someone even thought you don't like them or feel you can count on them for support, compassion and understanding.

CARPE DIEM:
Call a family member you feel close to today.
Make plans to visit this person soon.

86.

VISIT THE CEMETERY.

- Visiting the cemetery is an important mourning ritual. It helps us embrace our loss and remember the person who died.

- Memorial Day, Veteran's Day, Labor Day, and Mother's Day or Father's Day are traditional days to visit the cemetery and pay respects.

- If the body was cremated, you may want to visit the scattering site or columbarium.

- Sometimes in cases of sudden, violent death, a marker or memorial may be erected at the place of the death (e.g. the Oklahoma City bombing memorial). This can also be a sacred, healing place to visit and revisit.

- Ask a friend or family member to go with you. You may feel comforted by their presence. Or, if you are like me, you may find it more meaningful to go alone. Do what feels right for you.

CARPE DIEM:
If you can, drop by the cemetery today with a nosegay of fresh flowers. Scatter the petals over the grave.

87.

LET GO OF DESTRUCTIVE MYTHS ABOUT GRIEF AND MOURNING.

- You have probably internalized many of our society's harmful myths about grief and mourning.

  - Tears are a sign of weakness.
  - I need to get over my grief.
  - Death is something we don't talk about.
  - The more traumatic the death, the more I should try to put it behind me quickly and efficiently.
  - Other people need me so I need to "hurry up" and get back to my "normal" self.

- Sometimes these myths will cause you to feel guilty about or ashamed of your true thoughts and feelings.

- Your grief is your grief. It's normal and necessary. Allow it to be what it is.

CARPE DIEM:
Which grief myth has been most harmful to your grief journey? Consider the ways in which you can help teach others about these destructive myths.

88.

GET AWAY FROM IT ALL.

- Sometimes it takes a change of scenery to reveal the texture of our lives.

- New people and places help us see our lives from a new vantage point and can assist us in our search for meaning.

- Often, getting away from it all means leaving civilization behind and retreating to nature. But it can also mean temporarily abandoning your environment and spending time in one that's altogether different.

- Get away from it all every few hours by getting up, walking around, looking out the window and getting a drink of water. Take a reflective "time out" for several minutes.

- Visit a foreign country. Go backpacking in the wilderness. Spend a weekend at a monastery.

CARPE DIEM:
Plan a trip to somewhere far away. Ask a friend to travel with you. Just don't do this too soon; running away is not the same as getting away.

89.

IMAGINE THAT YOU WERE THERE WITH THE PERSON AS HE DIED.

- It's normal to think about the circumstances of a sudden, violent death. You may feel anguish that your loved one was in pain or afraid. You may feel despair that he was alone.

- It might comfort you to know that most people who are killed violently seem to suffer very little. The body's nervous system releases chemicals that create shock and block pain. Most people who are in a serious accident and live to tell about it report feeling and remembering almost nothing.

- If and when you are ready, it might also help you to imagine yourself holding and comforting the person as he died. A skilled counselor could help you through the process of imagining how you might have touched him and what you might have said. Play out the entire scene in your mind. Allow yourself to be there for him. Imagining this scenario may help you come to terms with some aspects of the death.

CARPE DIEM:

If it feels safe for you, draw a picture of the death. Insert yourself in this drawing, comforting and ministering to the person who died. Or draw an angel saving him from pain and lifting up his soul.

90.

RELEASE ANY BAD FEELINGS OR REGRETS YOU MAY HAVE ABOUT THE FUNERAL AND BURIAL.

- The funeral is a wonderful means of expressing our beliefs, thoughts and feelings about the death of someone loved.

- Funerals help us acknowledge the reality of the death, give testimony to the life of the person who died, express our grief, support each other, and embrace our faith and beliefs about life and death

- Yet for many survivors of sudden, violent death, funeral planning is difficult. Funeral and burial decisions may have been made quickly, while you were still in deep shock and disbelief. Sometimes some of these decisions seem wrong with the benefit of hindsight.

- If you harbor any negative feelings about the funeral or memorial service, know this: You and everyone else who was a part of the service did the best they could do at the time. You cannot change what happened, but you can talk about what happened and share your thoughts and feelings with someone who cares. Don't berate yourself.

- If you had a wonderful funeral, rejoice! Talk to someone about how meaningful it was to you.

- It's never too late to hold another memorial service. Perhaps a tree-planting ceremony or a small gathering on the anniversary of the death could be a forum for sharing memories and prayer. Ask a clergyperson or someone you know to be a good public speaker to help plan and lead the ceremony.

CARPE DIEM:

If you harbor regrets or anger about the funeral and burial, talk about these feelings with someone today. Perhaps the two of you together can create an "action plan" to help make things better.

91.

BELIEVE IN THE POWER OF STORY.

- Acknowledging a death is a painful, ongoing task that we accomplish in doses, over time. A vital part of healing in grief is often "telling the story" over and over again. For trauma survivors, the shock of the death may delay your need to talk about it for months, even years.

- In cases of sudden and violent death, you may feel compelled to think and talk about the circumstances of the death itself. This is normal and necessary. Your mind returns to the moment of the death in an effort to fathom that which is unfathomable. Telling the story is a natural way of trying to dissipate the psychic energy created by the trauma and trying to integrate the reality of what has happened.

- What if you don't want to talk about it? It's OK to respect this feeling for weeks or months, but soon you'll need to start talking about it. Keeping your thoughts and feelings about the death inside you only makes them more powerful. Giving them voice allows you some control over them. Trust that you will "tell your story" when you are ready.

- Over time, your grief story will likely evolve from one dominated by the death itself to one dominated by loving memories of the person who died. This is a natural progression and a sign that you are healing.

- Find people who are willing to listen to you tell your story, over and over again if necessary, without judgment. These are often "fellow strugglers" who have had similar losses. But remember that not everyone will be able to be a compassionate listener. Your story is a difficult one to hear. Seek out listeners who can be present to your pain.

CARPE DIEM:
Today, discuss the story of the death with someone else who loved the person who died. This person may also be struggling with painful questions and fears regarding the circumstances of the death. Listen to and support each other.

92.

TEACH OTHERS ABOUT GRIEF
AND MOURNING.

- To love is to one day mourn. You have learned this most poignant of life's lessons.

- Maybe you could teach what you are learning to others. Tell your friends and family about the six needs of mourning. Teach them about the unique aspects of traumatic grief. Teach them how they can best support you.

- Share your wisdom in the safety of a grief support group.

- Remember that each person's grief is unique. Your experiences will not be shared or appreciated by everyone.

CARPE DIEM:
Buy a friend the companion book to this one, called
Healing A Friend's Grieving Heart: 100 Practical Ideas for Helping Someone You Love Through Loss. It provides concise grief education and practical tips for helping.

93.

EXPRESS YOUR GRATITUDE.

- Despite the tragedy, you are probably grateful for many things in your life. When you feel mired in painful, sad feelings, try making a list of that for which you are grateful.

- You may be grateful for your children. For your spouse. For your siblings. For your parents. For your friends. You may be grateful for your job or your education. You might also try naming the little things that make you feel grateful: the way the sun danced on your countertop this morning; the peace you felt after going for a walk; the song you just heard on the radio.

- Don't forget to express your gratitude to those who offered help and comfort at the time of the death. Law enforcement personnel, medical workers, friends, even complete strangers may have gone above and beyond the call of duty to help you or someone in your family.

- Sometimes it helps to express your gratitude to the person who died. Write her a letter telling her what she meant to you and the lessons you learned from her. Tell her how grateful you are that her life, though too brief, was joined with yours.

CARPE DIEM:

Today, write a note of heartfelt gratitude to
someone you've neglected to thank.

94.

CHOOSE TO LIVE.

- Sudden, violent death often leaves mourners feeling powerless. You were powerless to prevent the death and you're powerless to reverse it. But you can regain a feeling of power by deciding to take control of the rest of your life.

- Will you merely exist for the remainder of your days or will you choose to truly live?

- Many mourners take up a new life direction after a sudden, violent death. Has the death given you a new perspective on life? How can you choose to act on this new perspective?

- What did the person who died love in life? How can you help nurture that love in the world in an ongoing, positive way?

- Sometimes choosing to live simply means living mindfully, with an appreciation for all that is good and beautiful and with a deep, a biding kindness to others.

- As a wise person once observed, "When old words die out on the tongue, new melodies spring forth from the heart."

CARPE DIEM:
Do one small thing today that demonstrates your
desire to live over merely existing.

95.

IMAGINE YOUR REUNION WITH THE PERSON WHO DIED.

- Most mourners I've talked to—and that number runs into the tens of thousands—are comforted by a belief or a hope that somehow, somewhere, the person who died lives on in health and happiness. For some, this belief is grounded in religious faith and the afterlife. For others it is simply a spiritual sense.

- If you believe in heaven, close your eyes and imagine what it might be like. Imagine the person who died strong and smiling. Imagine him doing what he enjoyed most in the company of loved ones who have gone before him.

- Some people have dreams in which the person who died seems to be communicating with them. Some feel the overwhelming presence of the person on occasion. Some actually "see" or "hear" the person. These are common, normal experiences and are often quite comforting.

CARPE DIEM:
If you believe in heaven or an afterlife (or even if you're not sure), imagine the reunion you may one day have with the person who died. Imagine the joy of being able to see, touch and talk to this person again. Imagine what you will say to one another.

96.

HELP OTHERS.

- Help others! But I'm the one who needs help right now, you may be thinking.

- It's true, you do deserve special compassion and attention right now. But often, people find healing in selflessness.

- When and only when you are ready, consider volunteering at a nursing home, a homeless shelter or your neighborhood school. If you try it and it seems to be too much, back off until you feel more able.

- If you're well into your grief journey, you may find yourself ready and able to help other mourners by starting a support group or volunteering at a hospice.

CARPE DIEM:
Do something nice for someone else today, maybe
someone who doesn't really deserve it.

97.

RESET YOUR CLOCK.

- When someone loved dies a sudden, violent death, there is only Before and After. There is your life Before the traumatic death and now there is your life After. It's as if your internal calendar gets reset to mark the significance of the profound loss.

- Many traumatized grievers can tell you, without thought or conscious calculation, how many years, months and days it has been since their loved one died.

- These new ways of keeping time are perfectly normal. You are not crazy! Your mind and heart have simply come up with a new system to mark the earth's relentless rotation.

- It's also OK to mention your new timekeeping system in everyday conversation: "Thanksgiving's coming. My brother died four Thanksgivings ago." Comments such as these let others know that it's important to you to remember and to continue to tell the story.

CARPE DIEM:

Write two columns on a piece of paper: Before and After. In ten minutes, brainstorm as many adjectives or feelings that you can think of that define each time period.

98.

REASSESS YOUR PRIORITIES.

- Death has a way of making us rethink our lives and the meaningfulness of the ways we spend them. The shock of sudden, violent death, especially, tends to awaken mourners to what is truly meaningful in life.

- What gives your life meaning? What doesn't? Take steps to spend more of your time on the former and less on the latter.

- Now may be the time to reconfigure your life. Choose a satisfying new career. Go back to school. Begin volunteering. Open yourself to potential new relationships. Help others in regular, ongoing ways. Move closer to your family.

- Many survivors of sudden, violent death have told me that they can no longer stand to be around people who seem shallow, egocentric, or mean-spirited. It's OK to let friendships wither with friends whom these adjectives now seem to describe. Instead, find ways to connect with people who share your new outlook on life—and death.

CARPE DIEM:
Make a list with two columns: What's important to me. What's not.
Brainstorm for at least 15 minutes.

99.

UNDERSTAND THE CONCEPT OF "RECONCILIATION."

- Sometimes you'll hear about "recovering" from grief. This term is damaging because it implies that grief is an illness that must be cured. It also connotes a return to the way things were before the death.

- We don't recover from grief. We become "reconciled" to it. In other words, we learn to live with it and are forever changed by it.

- This does not mean a life of misery, however. We often not only heal but grow through grief. Of course we are never glad that the person has died, but our lives can potentially be deeper and more meaningful after the death.

- Reconciliation takes time, especially after a sudden, violent death. You may not become truly reconciled to your loss for years and even then will have "griefbursts" (see Idea 52) forever.

- You will recognize that you are reconciling your grief when you again have the capacity to enjoy life and plan for the future. Your eating and sleeping habits will have stabilized. You will find yourself loving and being loved and nurturing your relationships with others. You will feel aware that while you will never "get over" your grief, your life does have a new reality, meaning and purpose.

- Perhaps you have heard it said that healing in grief is a journey, not a destination. While you will never "arrive," do be sure to have others continue to walk with you on the journey.

CARPE DIEM:
Think about the past losses in your life and the ways in which you've learned to reconcile yourself to them. This death will probably be harder for you to reconcile, but you can and you will.

100.

STRIVE TO GROW THROUGH GRIEF.

- Over time, you may find that you are growing emotionally and spiritually as a result of your grief journey. I understand that you've paid the ultimate price for this growth and that you would gladly trade it for one more minute with the person who died. Still, the death may have brought bittersweet gifts into your life that you would not otherwise have.

- Many mourners emerge from the early years of traumatic grief as stronger, more capable people. You may find that you're more assertive and apt to say what you really believe and be who you really are. You may no longer put up with baloney. You've already survived the worst life has to offer, so anything still to come can't be so bad. And you've learned what's truly important and what's not.

- What's more, many of you will discover depths of compassion for others that you never knew you had. Many survivors of sudden, violent death grow to volunteer, undertake daily kindnesses, become more emotionally and spiritually tuned-in to others and more interpersonally effective.

CARPE DIEM:
Consider the ways in which you may be "growing through grief."

A FINAL WORD

It is in suffering that we are withdrawn from the
bright superficial film of existence, from the sway of
time and mere things, and find ourselves in the
presence of a profounder truth.
Yves M. Congar
God, Man and the Universe

We have all heard the words "Blessed are those who mourn, for they
shall be comforted." To this I might add, "Blessed are those who
learn self-compassion during times of grief, for they shall go on to
discover continued meaning in life, living and loving."

I can't say enough about the importance of self-care as you experience
your traumatic grief. Remember—taking good care of yourself is not
selfish or self-indulgent. Instead, self-care fortifies you for the
ongoing ebbs and flows of your grief journey, a journey which leaves
you profoundly affected and deeply changed.

To be self-nurturing is to have the courage to pay attention to your
needs. Above all, self-nurturing is about self-acceptance. When we
recognize that self-care begins with ourselves, we no longer think of
those around as being totally responsible for our well-being. Healthy
self-care frees us to mourn in ways that help us heal, and that is
nurturing indeed.

I also believe self-nurturing is about celebration, taking time to enjoy
the moment, to find hidden treasures everywhere—a child's smile, a
beautiful sunrise, a flower in bloom, a friend's gentle touch. Grief
teaches us the importance of living fully in the present, remembering
our past, and embracing our future.

Walt Whitman wrote "I celebrate myself." In caring for yourself
"with passion" you are celebrating life as a human being who has been
touched by trauma and has come to recognize that the preciousness of
life is a superb opportunity for celebration!

Grief teaches us that there is so much to know about ourselves and the world around us. But to be open to that knowledge demands that we slow down, turn inward, and seek self-support as well as outside support.

Grief teaches us that we need to simplify our lives to be open to giving and receiving love. We need a sense of belonging, a sense of meaning, a sense of purpose. Realizing that we belong helps us feel safe and secure.

Grief teaches us we have only now to let people know that we love them. There are magic and miracles in loving and being loved. One final "carpe diem" for you: Call someone right now and let them know how their kindness and love sustain you.

Bless you. I hope we meet one day.

THE MOURNER'S CODE

Ten Self-Compassionate Principles

Though you should reach out to others as you journey through grief, you should not feel obligated to accept the unhelpful responses you may receive from some people. You are the one who is grieving, and as such, you have certain "rights" no one should try to take away from you.

The following list is intended both to empower you to heal and to decide how others can and cannot help. This is not to discourage you from reaching out to others for help, but rather to assist you in distinguishing useful responses from hurtful ones.

1. You have the right to experience your own unique grief.
No one else will grieve in exactly the same way you do. So, when you turn to others for help, don't allow them to tell what you should or should not be feeling.

2. You have the right to talk about your grief.
Talking about your grief will help you heal. Seek out others who will allow you to talk as much as you want, as often as you want, about your grief. If at times you don't feel like talking, you also have the right to be silent.

3. You have the right to feel a multitude of emotions.
Confusion, numbness, disorientation, fear, guilt and relief are just a few of the emotions you might feel as part of your grief journey. Others may try to tell you that feeling angry, for example, is wrong. Don't take these judgmental responses to heart. Instead, find listeners who will accept your feelings without condition.

4. You have the right to be tolerant of your physical and emotional limits.
Your feelings of loss and sadness will probably leave you feeling fatigued. Respect what your body and mind are telling you. Get daily rest. Eat balanced meals. And don't allow others to push you into doing things you don't feel ready to do.

5. You have the right to experience "griefbursts."
Sometimes, out of nowhere, a powerful surge of grief may overcome you. This can be frightening, but is normal and natural. Find someone who understands and will let you talk it out.

6. You have the right to make use of ritual.
The funeral ritual does more than acknowledge the death of someone loved. It helps provide you with the support of caring people. More importantly, the funeral is a way for you to mourn. If others tell you the funeral or other healing rituals such as these are silly or unnecessary, don't listen.

7. You have the right to embrace your spirituality.
If faith is a part of your life, express it in ways that seem appropriate to you. Allow yourself to be around people who understand and support your religious beliefs. If you feel angry at God, find someone to talk with who won't be critical of your feelings of hurt and abandonment.

8. You have the right to search for meaning.
You may find yourself asking, "Why did he or she die? Why this way? Why now?" Some of your questions may have answers, but some may not. And watch out for the clichéd responses some people may give you. Comments like, "It was God's will" or "Think of what you have to be thankful for" are not helpful and you do not have to accept them.

9. You have the right to treasure your memories.
Memories are one of the best legacies that exist after the death of someone loved. You will always remember. Instead of ignoring your memories, find others with whom you can share them.

10. You have the right to move toward your grief and heal.
Reconciling your grief will not happen quickly. Remember, grief is a process, not an event. Be patient and tolerant with yourself and avoid people who are impatient and intolerant with you. Neither you nor those around you must forget that the death of someone loved changes your life forever.

SEND US YOUR IDEAS
FOR HEALING YOUR
TRAUMATIZED HEART!

I'd love to hear you practical ideas for being self-compassionate in grief. I may use them in future editions of this book or in other publications through the Center for Loss. Please jot down your idea and mail it to:

Dr. Alan Wolfelt
The Center for Loss and transition
3735 Broken Bow Rd.
Fort Collins, CO 80526
wolfelt@centerforloss.com

I look forward to hearing from you!

My idea:

_____

_____

_____

_____

_____

_____

_____

My name and mailing address:

_____

_____

_____

ALSO BY ALAN WOLFELT

THE JOURNEY THROUGH GRIEF: REFLECTIONS ON HEALING

This spiritual guide to those grieving the death of someone loved explores the mourner's journey through grief, in particular the six needs that all mourners must meet to heal and grow. Following a short explanation of each mourning need are a series of short reflections written to help mourners work on each need as they feel ready.

Bound in hardcover and designed with grace, *The Journey Through Grief* is a much-loved, often-referred-to companion on many mourners' bedside tables.

"A gem to be treasured as well as a compassionate, spiritual harvest of redemptive truths and an affirming message of faith, hope and healing."
Rabbi Earl A. Grollman
Author of *Living When a Loved One Has Died*

"Dr. Wolfelt reminds us that it is not only the physical and emotional but also the spiritual that needs to be explored in the journeys through grief. Stirring and abundantly encouraging to all mourners."
Ros Crichton and Glen Crichton
Directors, COPING Bereavment Support Groups of Ontario

ISBN 1-879651-11-4 • 160 pages • Hardcover • $19.95
(plus additional shipping and handling)

Companion
P R E S S

All Dr. Wolfelt's publications can be ordered by mail from:
Companion Press
3735 Broken Bow Road • Fort Collins, CO 80526
(970) 226-6050 • Fax 1-800-922-6051
www.centerforloss.com

ALSO BY ALAN WOLFELT

HEALING A FRIEND'S GRIEVING HEART: 100 PRACTICAL IDEAS FOR HELPING SOMEONE YOU LOVE THROUGH LOSS

When a friend suffers the loss of someone loved, you may not always know what to say: But you can do many helpful, loving things"Compassionate and eminently practical, Healing A Friend's Grieving Heart offers 100 fresh ideas for supporting a grieving friend or family member. Some of the ideas teach the fundamentals of grief and mourning, while others offer practical day-to-day ways to help. Turn to any page and seize the day by being a real friend in grief today, right now, right this minute.

ISBN 1-879651-26-2
128 pages • Softcover • $11.95
(plus additional shipping and handling)

Companion
PRESS

All Dr. Wolfelt's publications can be ordered by mail from:
Companion Press
3735 Broken Bow Road • Fort Collins, CO 80526
(970) 226-6050 • Fax 1-800-922-6051
www.centerforloss.com

ALSO BY ALAN WOLFELT

HEALING A PARENT'S GRIEVING HEART: 100 PRACTICAL IDEAS AFTER YOUR CHILD DIES

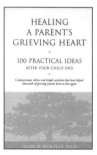

The unthinkable happened: your child has died. How do you go on? What can you do with your pain? Where do you turn?

With a forward by bereaved parent and editor of Bereavement Magazine Andrea Gambill, this book offers 100 practical ideas that have helped other grieving parents understand and reconcile their grief. Common challenges, such as dealing with marital stress, helping surviving siblings, dealing with hurtful advice from others and exploring feelings of guilt, are also addressed.

ISBN 1-879651-30-0
128 pages • Softcover • $11.95
(plus additional shipping and handling)

Companion
PRESS

All Dr. Wolfelt's publications can be ordered by mail from:
Companion Press
3735 Broken Bow Road • Fort Collins, CO 80526
(970) 226-6050 • Fax 1-800-922-6051
www.centerforloss.com

ALSO BY ALAN WOLFELT

HEALING A CHILD'S GRIEVING HEART:100 PRACTICAL IDEAS FOR FAMILIES, FRIENDS & CAREGIVERS

An idea book for grown-ups who what practical, day-to-day "how tos" for helping the grieving children they love. Some ideas teach about children's unique mourning styles and needs. Others suggest simple activities and tips for spending time together.

ISBN 1-879651-28-9
128 pages • Softcover • $11.95
(plus additional shipping and handling)

Companion
PRESS

All Dr. Wolfelt's publications can be ordered by mail from:
Companion Press
3735 Broken Bow Road • Fort Collins, CO 80526
(970) 226-6050 • Fax 1-800-922-6051
www.centerforloss.com

ALSO BY ALAN WOLFELT

HEALING YOUR GRIEVING HEART FOR KIDS:100 PRACTICAL IDEAS

Simple advice and activities for children after a death. An idea book for young and middle readers (6-12 year-olds) grieving the death of someone loved. The text is simple and straightforward, teaching children about grief and affirming that their thoughts and feelings are not only normal but necessary. Page after page of age-appropriate activities and gentle, healing guidance.

ISBN 1-879651-27-0
128 pages • Softcover • $11.95
(plus additional shipping and handling)

Companion
PRESS

All Dr. Wolfelt's publications can be ordered by mail from:
Companion Press
3735 Broken Bow Road • Fort Collins, CO 80526
(970) 226-6050 • Fax 1-800-922-6051
www.centerforloss.com

ALSO BY ALAN WOLFELT

HEALING A TEEN'S GRIEVING HEART:100 PRACTICAL IDEAS FOR FAMILIES, FRIENDS & CAREGIVERS

If you want to help a grieving teen but aren't sure how, this book is for you. It explains the teen's unique mourning needs, offers real-world advice and suggests realistic activities.

ISBN 1-879651-24-6
128 pages • Softcover • $11.95
(plus additional shipping and handling)

Companion
P R E S S

All Dr. Wolfelt's publications can be ordered by mail from:
Companion Press
3735 Broken Bow Road • Fort Collins, CO 80526
(970) 226-6050 • Fax 1-800-922-6051
www.centerforloss.com

ALSO BY ALAN WOLFELT

HEALING YOUR GRIEVING HEART FOR TEENS:100 PRACTICAL IDEAS

Grief is especially difficult during the teen years. This book explains why this is so and offers straightforward, practical advice for healing

ISBN 1-879651-23-8
128 pages • Softcover • $11.95
(plus additional shipping and handling)

Companion
PRESS

All Dr. Wolfelt's publications can be ordered by mail from:
Companion Press
3735 Broken Bow Road • Fort Collins, CO 80526
(970) 226-6050 • Fax 1-800-922-6051
www.centerforloss.com

ALSO BY ALAN WOLFELT

HEALING THE ADULT CHILD'S GRIEVING HEART: 100 PRACTICAL IDEAS AFTER YOUR PARENT DIES

When people get older, they die. We understand this, yet when a parent who has lived to middle or old age dies, the death often still comes as a shock. And the grief can be surprisingly deep and painful. Why do adult children whose parent has died often feel "orphaned," depressed and alone? What should they do with their sadness, resentment or anger? What are some effective ways to cope?

Written by Dr. Wolfelt and including his own personal insights since the death of his father, this book offers 100 practical ideas that have helped many adult children come to understand and reconcile their grief. Common challenges, such as helping the surviving parent, resolving sibling conflicts, and dealing with legal and financial issues, are also addressed.

Whether your parent died in middle or old age, whether the death was sudden or anticipated, this compassionate and easy-to-use resource is for you. Turn to any page and seize the day by taking a small step towards healing.

ISBN 1-879651-31-9
128 pages • Softcover • $11.95
(plus additional shipping and handling)

Companion
PRESS

All Dr. Wolfelt's publications can be ordered by mail from:
Companion Press
3735 Broken Bow Road • Fort Collins, CO 80526
(970) 226-6050 • Fax 1-800-922-6051
www.centerforloss.com

ALSO BY ALAN WOLFELT

THE HEALING YOUR GRIEVING HEART JOURNAL FOR TEENS

Teenagers often don't want to talk to adults—or even to their friends—about their struggles. But given the opportunity, many will choose the more private option of writing. Many grieving teens find that journaling helps them sort through their confusing thoughts and feelings.

Yet few journals created just for teens exist and even fewer address the unique needs of the grieving teen. In the Introduction, this unique journal affirms the grieving teen's journey and offers gentle, healing guidance. Then, throughout, the authors provide simple, open-ended questions for the grieving teen to explore.

To encourage free expression, other pages in the journal are blank or simply provide brief, life-affirming quotes from the world's greatest thinkers.

Designed just for grieving teens as a companion to Dr. Wolfelt's bestselling *Healing Your Grieving Heart for Teens: 100 Practical Ideas*, this journal will be a comforting, affirming and healing presence for teens in the weeks, months and years after the death of someone loved.

ISBN 1-879651-33-5
128 pages • Softcover • $11.95
(plus additional shipping and handling)

Companion
P R E S S

All Dr. Wolfelt's publications can be ordered by mail from:
Companion Press
3735 Broken Bow Road • Fort Collins, CO 80526
(970) 226-6050 • Fax 1-800-922-6051
www.centerforloss.com